BONKERS: THE STORY OF
DIZZEE RASCAL

D1339435

BONKERS: THE STORY OF DIZZEE RASCAL

PAUL LESTER

OMNIBUS PRESS

London / New York / Paris / Sydney / Copenhagen / Berlin / Madrid / Tokyo

Exclusive Distributors
Music Sales Limited,
14/15 Berners Street,
London, W1T 3LJ.

Music Sales Corporation,
257 Park Avenue South,
New York, NY 10010, USA.

Macmillan Distribution Services,
56 Parkwest Drive
Derrimut, Vic 3030,
Australia.

Every effort has been made to trace the copyright holders of the photographs in this book but one or two were unreachable. We would be grateful if the photographers concerned would contact us.

Typeset by: Phoenix Photosetting, Chatham, Kent
Printed in the E.U.

A catalogue record for this book is available from the British Library.

Visit Omnibus Press on the web at www.omnibuspress.com

Contents

CHAPTER 1

Jus' A Rascal

"Music was the only option open to me. It was a blessing I pursued it. I didn't care about no other subjects. I'd have just ended up carrying on a life of crime, I suppose. Where I'm from, there ain't a lot of other options."

Dizzee Rascal

Dizzee Rascal, along with Tricky the most original black British musician of the last two decades, was born Dylan Kwabena Mills on October 1, 1985. He grew up on a council estate in Bow, east London, and if that wasn't tough enough, his Nigerian father died when he was two. This meant that his Ghanaian mother, Priscilla, had to bring up her baby son alone.

Even after Dizzee had made it, and become arguably the biggest male solo pop star in Britain, he still wasn't exactly sure what the circumstances were of his father's death. "There's obviously something that's gone on that's been kept from me," he told Ben Thompson of *The Daily Telegraph* in 2009. He further explained that it was a subject that his mother felt disinclined to discuss, even if he did find it difficult growing up not knowing what had happened.

"I don't have any memories of him at all," he said, explaining the problems he experienced growing up with just one parent. "It was definitely difficult when I was young – you play the cards you're dealt, but obviously something like that can shape the choices you make in life. I definitely had a problem with authority. I just remember feeling really suppressed at school. I think a lot of young black boys feel that way growing up. Whether it's being poor, and just not understanding, kind of, why you? Whatever the reason, you end up lashing out. There's so much that you take until eventually you just say, 'Fuck it!'"

Not knowing his father, or the circumstances of his death, aggravated the normal sense of confusion felt by most children. But Dizzee has admitted: "I've got over it and just got on with life. And now I've built up enough of an identity for myself that I don't even need to pursue it any more."

If he was unable to recall his father, the memories that he retains of his mother from his childhood couldn't be more vivid. He describes her as "full-on", and acknowledges that "she did the best she could", adding that "she beat me when she had to". However, he has nothing but respect for her. "The older I get, the more I love and respect my mum for how she managed to raise me up and carry me through," he told *The Daily Telegraph*. He remembers her studying law to be a legal secretary, and generally doing whatever work it took to see her and her son through. This involved holding down two jobs at once, sometimes three. "Any honest thing possible to make money, she did – cleaning jobs, selling clothes on the estate where we lived, packing envelopes, being an Avon lady," recalled Dizzee. "She worked and worked and worked to put food on the table and pay the child minder, and she never missed a parents' evening."

Priscilla Mills made the young Dylan realise how important it was to have a serious work ethic. He told *The Student Pocket Guide*: "I had a good mum, man; she did a lot for me. She showed me and she's a big part of how I look at life, just working hard no matter what. Do you know what? I never saw my mum sit there and just lie about and get benefits or nothing like that. Even when she was ill she would go to work. The closest person to me never gave up and it would take a lot [for her] to even take a day off."

She also inculcated in him a sense of the importance of discipline and devotion, encouraging him to accompany her to church; she would attend several of east London's black-led churches – "mainly Pentecostal ones with a choir, like you see in America," he explained. Over time, visiting church on a Sunday went from being a pleasure to an obligation to a chore, and Dizzee would eventually refuse to go, although looking back today he remembers enjoying the experience and appreciates what his mother was trying to do. "I'm glad she made me go," he has said, "because I think that's where my independence has come from, more than anything – from my mum and the church." He reiterated the point to Ed Marriot in *The Times* when he spoke of the inner strength that was the result of his religious faith: "I was raised in the Church and, yeah, I pray sometimes," he said. "But I talk to God in my own way, and my own time."

That feeling of independence increased as his busy working mother would have to leave her son at a babysitter, or he would be left to fend for himself when she invariably came home from work exhausted. Without a father around, early on Dizzee realised that he would have to become the man of the house himself. "I grew up and learnt to hold my own," he said. "My mum was doing two people's jobs. It makes you grow up early. There's less people to talk to, less close people, innit? You're going to end up being lonely because you think a bit more. I had to learn to be a man myself."

He may have been forced to become an adult while still an adolescent, but that didn't mean he wasn't prone to bouts of delinquency of the juvenile variety, at home and around the estate, as well as at school. As a fatherless only child, he was, in his words, "a bit of a naughty boy". This is something of an understatement considering that his disruptive behaviour – including hurling chairs at, and fighting with, teachers – led to him being expelled from four different schools in as many years. There was, however, one upside to all this negative interaction with authority – it was a teacher at one of his schools who, exposed to his random acts of transgression, first referred to him using the name that would one day become his stage and recording alias, 'Rascal'.

"I was a violent kid for a start," he told Tim Adams of *The Observer* in 2009. "A lot of fighting. Probably I had to prove something. There was no man in my house, the classic story. It was quite a tough estate. Not the worst. But you needed to look after yourself from primary school on."

Dizzee has spoken at length about his directionless childhood and adolescence, putting his teen misdemeanours down to simple frustration. The term he used for himself was a "hoodrat" – inner-London speak for troublemaker – even though he knew he had the wherewithal to achieve more. "I liked the streets more than school so I would always bunk off," he has said. "I've always been troublesome. I was one of those kids that couldn't get on with anyone. I never liked school, never liked anyone telling me what to do. Now I'm older I understand that you have to take orders to get anywhere. The worst thing was that I was smart, which meant I didn't get what I should've out of it."

He spoke further about his criminal past to the *Financial Times* in 2007. "Basically I was part of the crime wave in my area," he explained. "They put up signs in train stations because of kids like me. I've still got friends that are going through some situations. I can never forget where I'm from." Yet even this early on, it was clear that he intended to pursue a different direction. "By the time my friends dabbled in the whole crack [cocaine] thing when we were 16 or 17, I was making money from music. So that kind of let me be around them, but also kick back and really see what the gangster life was about. The early mornings, maybe some of the kidnappings, the this, the that, the dropping offs, the crack dens, the crackheads coming out of nowhere, all the not-so-nice shit, the Feds putting guns to your head on the floor, random stoppings, all the bullshit. So I got to see that early."

The early Noughties saw a spate of teenage murders in the capital, focusing media attention on violence among black youth.

"This ain't nothing I ain't seen, but now the world's caught on to it," he told the *Financial Times*. "I've got friends that, when they were 14, 15, they got stabbed as well."

For a while, it looked as though Dylan Mills might follow that same route. He was clever but undisciplined at school. "I was in the top classes, I was up there, but then my behaviour would slip – boredom, frustration and issues – so I shouted at the world." If he was out of control at school, at home he used music to express his confusion and frustration, blasting out drum'n'bass and US rap, as well as, less predictably, punk and heavy metal – anything extreme. His mother's beloved gospel music fought for airspace with the noise from his favourite local pirate radio stations. He would surprise classmates by performing Nirvana songs at school concerts; he even read rock magazine *Kerrang!* and infuriated his friends by blasting out his favourite hard rock tracks whenever they played football outside his bedroom window. "People thought I was crazy," he admitted later on, "and I was an attention-seeker, but I always loved that music, and I was serious about trying to make them like it."

Meanwhile, out on the streets, there were numerous examples of what Dizzee has termed his youthful "madnesses – joyriding, street crime, violent disorder". He explained that it was partly out of sheer boredom. "I didn't have a job and I'd just run around and do shit that you see people doing," he said. Hardly proud of his antics, he is nevertheless honest about what he got up to. "I was wild, but I wasn't an organised criminal. There's a degree of skill involved in it – there must be as I was never caught. I don't wanna justify it – it was like a phase. It's easy to copy what you see around you – it's all about peer pressure."

Often, he would take the Docklands Light Railway a few stops from Bow towards Stratford where, at the Three Flats tower blocks, he would hang about, smoke, steal cars and pizzas from pizza delivery boys. As he reminisced in *The Student Pocket Guide*: "I stole a few cars but it was just a phase I was going through. That pizza man thing, people talk like it was like a career. It wasn't a career, I just lived on the estate, and it was a normal thing. The pizza man would come and you just go and take the pizza, innit – you know, out of the box on the bike."

His general view of his wild teenage years was that "there was a lot of mess about it; it was rough and violent. I had to learn a lot of lessons early. I went kind of off the rails at a certain age. When you see what's going on around you, you start taking part in it." He added: "When I got to that age, I was independent; I could look after myself early. I used to go and get money myself, or if I wanted to do something I'd be determined and I'd go and do it." He also said that he and his friends would "fight with kids from other estates", although he compared his relatively harmless disputes with more dangerous contemporary altercations, which are settled using handguns.

One of his regrets from this period in his life is that he caused his hard-working, conscientious mother considerable aggravation and heartache. "I put her through a lot of hassle to be honest," he told a journalist. "She is nothing like me; she's a good woman, you know?"

Dizzee was saved from the proverbial life of crime by one of the subjects at his fifth and final school – Langdon Park Secondary School in Tower Hamlets, east London. There, despite quite enjoying Information Technology (IT) and English, he was, as he had been at his previous schools, excluded from most lessons on the curriculum. Either that or he was the pupil most likely to be chastised in the classroom – the boy in the corner, as his 2003 début album title had it. So he sought solace in the school's music room, where he finally found a creative focus for all his anger and energy (he had, around the same time, one other outlet for his artistic ambitions – he used to attend YATI: The Young Actors Theatre Islington).

It was a teacher at Langdon Park, Tim Smith, who recognised in Dylan Mills a nascent talent and found a way to nurture it without alienating the learning-averse pupil. Eventually, Smith would mentor him into securing an A in his music GCSE, the only exam he passed, while in return Dizzee would honour his former teacher on the sleeve of his début album, *Boy In Da Corner*.

Around this time, Mr Smith spoke to music website ukmusic. com about his stellar ex-pupil, about his unique personality, and the techniques he employed that made him stand out from his peers in the playground. "He came into the classroom really knowing what he wanted to do," Smith said of Mills. "The way he went about it was so different from what other students did, it stood out and had the wow factor." As advice to future young Dizzee Rascals out there, Smith suggested they check out a piece of downloadable software on the internet called Cakewalk that "will allow you to start creating rhythmic tracks even without a keyboard to do it, using a paintbrush". He also stressed, perhaps thinking of the highly astute Dylan Mills, the importance of developing one's "critical awareness" and being "willing to make change". He also hinted that some of Dizzee's music-room experiments may have featured Smith's own touches – "Some of his early stuff had a bit of me in there" – and suggested a future collaboration was not out of the question. "I'd love to in the future," he joked, "but who knows?"

Smith and Mills also paid tribute to each other – after the latter won the prestigious Mercury Music Prize for his ground-breaking 2003 début LP – in separate interviews for an article in the now-defunct *Observer Music Monthly* magazine. Smith, head of arts at Langdon Park when Dizzee Rascal was a pupil and later head of arts at Kidbrooke School in south London, went first. He explained that at Langdon Park, a well-equipped school in a deprived area, they were fortunate enough to have "incredible access to computers and generous funding from local businesses" and would acquire computers that had been discarded by companies at nearby Canary Wharf.

He remembered that, when he first came into his music class, Mills was 14 years old and in Year 10. There was no trepidation on his part – Smith admitted he never had a problem with Mills' behaviour despite his reputation, and never experienced his locally notorious "attitude". Smith's aim was always to emphasise to all and sundry his music skills, and luckily in this he had the backing of a very supportive head teacher. And if ever his mother did get called into the school regarding some minor indiscretion or other on her son's part, the teacher would make sure he met up with her afterwards and play her his latest composition, "to cheer her up".

He marvelled in *OMM* about how quick Dylan was to learn – in his very first music lesson he immediately set about completing a task on a computer using the Cubase music software program. "He used me and the other staff to explain things but he didn't need much help," said Smith. "He knew what he wanted to achieve and he worked quickly. He was noticeably better than the others because his music had a clear structure and pattern, an amazing balance between rhythm, bass and melody."

According to Smith, Dizzee's talent was fully formed from the start – the sounds that came blaring out of the Langdon Park music room were not dissimilar to the avant-garde grime that would eventually comprise the noise on his *Boy In Da Corner* album four years later. Indeed, it was in the music room that he wrote his first hit, 'I Luv U', a sharp burst of grime *vérité* concerning teenage pregnancy and abortion. "When I listen to [his early music] I can visualise exactly how it would appear on the computer screen," Smith told *OMM*, revealing that he still had in his possession 33 tracks that Mills had made while at school: "Some of them are works in progress," he said, "but most stand out as very interesting." He also noted the similarity between Dizzee's early forays and the work of highbrow minimalist composers such as John Adams and Philip Glass, perhaps because, as a fan of their compositions, Smith would regularly play them to his pupil. "There is a similar feel to some of the music Dizzee composed on Cubase. I remember bringing their music to his attention, although he was never short of inspiration."

Dizzee was next to speak in *OMM*'s two-way appreciation society, explaining that, because he took an instant liking to the teacher, in Mr Smith's lessons he "never had an attitude". He especially appreciated being left to his own devices, granting him the time, space and freedom to work on tracks using the equipment in the music room – notably, a computer, a mixer, a mini-disc recorder, a CD recorder and a printer. Dizzee would be so engrossed that he would work through playtime and lunchtime. "It was the only place in school that I actually wanted to be," he told *OMM*. "I was focused and I didn't worry about what else was going on. I played music as

I'd always imagined hearing it in my head." It didn't even bother him that Smith was a middle-aged man; there was a mutual respect that transcended the age barrier. "He understood my music and understood what I was trying to do, so nothing else mattered. If he suggested that I listen to something I would. Sometimes he gave me music or videos to watch as well." Without his help and inspiration, Dizzee's school days would have been far less enjoyable, and his life might have turned out quite differently. "School would have been pretty dead really for me without music," he confessed. "Everything started there; I mastered my style in that little back room."

As a musician he might have been raw and untutored, and technically speaking he may have been lacking in proficiency, but his music bore the self-assurance of a young man who had a particular sound in his head, and some idea of how he intended to realise it. "I don't really class myself as a musician," he said. "I can make music but I'm not the greatest technically. There were other people who were technically better than me in school, but I knew how I wanted to sound and all I needed was to work out how to do it."

Most importantly, notwithstanding certain deficiencies in terms of expertise, Dizzee had an idiosyncratic vision, and an original voice, that would prove to be his passport out of the dead end that was his education and council estate upbringing. "In the end," he told Alexis Petridis of *The Guardian* in 2003, "music was the only option open to me. It was a blessing I pursued it. I put all my energies into it. I didn't care about no other subjects. I'd have just ended up carrying on a life of crime, I suppose. I would have done anything to get money. Where I'm from, there ain't a lot of other options, you know what I'm saying? Entertainment or football or crime." Not that Dizzee wanted to propagate the idea that music and sport – and crime – were the only options, because if the success that he would eventually enjoy taught him anything, it was that there were no limits to what a young person could achieve, given the right level of ambition and self-belief. "I don't want to spread the message that all you can do is music or sport," he said. "You can be anything. Anything. That's the message I like to spread."

CHAPTER 2

Paranoid

"There is nothing worse than being clever or creative and having no outlet, or being in peer groups where people think you are weird if you want to work hard at something."

Nick Cage

The teenage Dylan Mills had been such a source of anxiety to his mother that there were times when friends and relations felt as though there was only one solution. As he said: "There were times when people said that she should send me to Africa, because I was a lost cause, but she stuck with it..."

Fortunately, he had supportive people around him to keep him on the straight and narrow. An amateur psychologist might surmise that Mills, lacking a father figure or indeed any positive male role model in his life, sought out strong older men from whom to seek guidance and inspiration as he teetered perilously close to going off the rails.

One such character was Daniel 'Danny' Shittu, the Nigerian footballer, born in 1980, who began his career playing for the then-Premier League side Charlton Athletic in 1999. Mills and Shittu were childhood friends, the former, a supporter of West Ham United, describing him as "like a big brother".

"I don't think I was ever really a normal kid," said Dizzee later on. "I always wanted to do it big, and so I was always on the lookout for strong people I could learn from. I suppose wanting a father figure was a part of that, but it was also that I was always searching for something more." Speaking about Shittu after he became famous, Dizzee regretted not giving him more credit for looking out for him at Langdon Park School and elsewhere, and for encouraging him early on to pursue his love of music: "Danny is someone I should've mentioned a lot more, really," he said. "He had the turntables, so when I first started making tracks or putting mix-tapes together, it would usually be at his house."

Of course, one other surrogate father in the teenage Dylan Mills' life was his Langdon Park School teacher Tim Smith. It was Smith who gave him access, via the school's music room, to the equipment with which he would make his first recordings. The teacher would, on Monday nights, allow the pupil and his friends from the local area to come into the music department after school so that they could work on tracks together. He would organise visits for Mills to the professional studio across the road from the school, where he could receive proper hands-on experience of the technology he would use, and the skills he would require, to make a record. Smith even arranged for him to attend, during the school holidays, a music workshop run by Tower Hamlets' Summer University (of which Dizzee would later become a patron).

When he was 12, that other positive role model in Dizzee's life, his mother, bought him his first ever set of turntables so that he wouldn't have to borrow Danny Shittu's any more, and although she was pleased to see him developing a serious interest, she didn't quite believe those decks would be the first step on the road to chart success.

"She bought my first turntable, but I don't think she knew how deep I was getting into music until she saw me on TV," he told Gavin Martin of the *Daily Mirror* later on. It was only when Dizzee started cropping up on mainstream television shows several years down the line that she knew her patience with her handful of a son had truly paid off. "As long as she's happy," he said to Martin, joking: "I bought her the house she lives in, so you'd hope she thinks it's worthwhile."

According to Dizzee, even aged 12 he was "deadly serious" about making music on his turntables – friends would come over to his house, where they would make tapes. He was also, at this young age, already writing and recording his own material, as well as skiving off school to do stints as an amateur DJ and MC at small east London youth-club garage raves. His school life, understandably, suffered as a consequence, as he later told US magazine *Blender*. "I'd go to school in the morning, and I was so tired," he said. "So I stopped giving a shit about lessons. I used to bunk off and do music." He added, much to the puzzlement of the American journalist, more used to "y'knows" from US rappers than "innits": "These last three years, I haven't had a lot of sleep, innit? We was doing raves from when I was 16, 17 – going up and down the country, sometimes doing two or three raves in one night. I was always coming home at six o'clock in the morning. I'm sure my mum thought I was selling drugs." At this time, Dizzee would pay to get into raves and hang about "looking for my chance to get on the mic," as he reminisced in *The Observer*. "There's no point waiting around being polite: you've got to grab it and tell 'em, 'I'm next.'" He further explained on music website UK Music that he would just turn up at raves, mostly of the youth club variety, pay to get in if necessary, and proceed to "get on the mic and MC". It was trial by fire. "That's where all the grimy people are, the ones where you can go wrong," he said. "If people don't feel you they'll show you."

It is said that his ambition to be an MC on a local pirate radio station was somewhat hindered by his idiosyncratic delivery, his high-pitched staccato "flow" (or rather, non-flow – it was arrhythmic, sharp, and it came at you in shards), even though this would later become his signature sound, his calling card, following the release of

Boy In Da Corner. Nevertheless, he gave it a shot. A dangerous one at that: according to an interview that he gave to Nick Hasted of *The Independent* in 2003, Dizzee "MC'd first as a hobby" before it "became an obsession: he would shimmy up the sides of buildings with pirate radio wires in his mouth, in return for air-time".

He tried his luck broadcasting until the early hours of the morning on smaller north London stations for months before going for bigger and more prestigious stations, with a wider reach, where the likes of Wiley, Pay As U Go Cartel, Roll Deep Crew and More Fire Crew made their names as local heroes. The intrepid Dizzee targeted one pirate station in particular, hoping it would be the place that would further his career: Rinse FM, which used to broadcast from the Stratford Three Flats tower blocks that were once his stamping ground. It did indeed play its part in his irresistible rise, but just not in the way that he expected – he wanted to be a DJ there; they ended up playing his own recordings, and the station can be credited with helping to launch his career as a solo artist.

The influential pirate broadcaster celebrated its 15th birthday in 2009, when it was described by *Dummy* magazine as "the most important British radio station of the last 15 years" (in June 2010, it was finally granted a legal broadcasting licence). Started out by DJ Geeneus, the station gave artists like Digital Mystikz and Wiley, another Dizzee mentor, a platform well before grime became a commercial proposition. It was to Rinse that Dizzee Rascal sent an audition tape, in the vain hope that he would be taken on as a drum'n'bass DJ. It's not known what the station – regarded as a prime mover in the creation and development of grime and dubstep – made of the tape, and it's unclear whether he was allowed to do any broadcasting there, although reports suggest that he did have his own slot on Rinse FM. As Dizzee has said, "Doing that stuff, I could be at one with myself, get into a zone, and then create something. I loved that feeling. That buzz was more addictive to me than anything on the planet."

He discussed this period with Emma Warren of *Dummy* magazine. She asked him what kind of DJ he was, whether he was just "the kid doing loads of shouts out to his mates" or simply playing music? Replied Dizzee, who at the time would broadcast under the name Dizzy D: "I was a joke! I was clowning. I had decks and that in my bedroom, so people'd come to my yard to make tapes or listen to tunes. I didn't care that much about MCing. It actually started because I'd be DJing, grabbing the mic, mucking around, then getting back on the decks. People started to take the piss out of you more and more, and that made me do it more. That was me up to about the age of 12. Then I started writing lyrics," he added, revealing that his first set of words were about comic-book superhero Spider-Man. He further explained that his intention wasn't at this point to be "a massive MC" but a DJ, even if fate took him in a different direction. "The whole thing just happened because I wasn't any good at it," he said. "So I'd just grab the mic off people."

It was when he was 17 years old that Dizzee knew for sure that his days in education were truly over and that he fully intended to pursue music as a career. As he told *The Student Pocket Guide*: "I dropped out of college when I was 17 and I think from there that's when it seriously took over and I thought, 'I ain't going to college no more. I'm gonna be in the studio all of the time and I'm gonna go to all the raves.'" Considering that, within a year, he would have a record deal with leading British indie label XL, the home of The Prodigy, it could reasonably be argued that Dizzee was right to choose music over further education. During this period, while he was attempting to break into pirate radio and appearing at raves (places such as Caesars, Stratford Rex, The Palace Pavilion – what Dizzee termed "the gutter raves", telling Emma Warren of *Dummy* magazine, "I couldn't even get into the garage raves. I didn't have the clothes or the attitude"), he was still sometimes guilty of indulging in petty misdemeanours, from joy-riding to street robbery; "my little stints of illegal bullshit", as he called them. Then again, perhaps he should be allowed some leeway for being a product of east London's estates. As Dizzee has said, "Growing up there shaped me to an extent. It makes your outlook narrower – you've got less opportunity."

But in a way his occasional lapses into delinquency made him all the more determined to focus completely on his music. "I wasn't proud – that's why I got out quick and did something honest instead," he said, emphasising the importance of finding an alternative, an escape route, a way out. "I don't know the answers to all the problems there [ie Bow in east London], but for individuals, I'd say, 'Find something that you want to do and chase it until you get it. Music was what I chased." He added that, "To an extent music has saved me because it was the right choice to make. It came to a time when it was like, 'What is the point of all this bullshit anyway?' Then I just stuck solely with the music."

When asked later on what his advice would be to a teenager in a similar predicament to the one in which he found himself, torn between a life of crime and the more risky pursuit of one's dreams, he replied: "You have to make music your life. Everything that you think you have got on the sideline is just taking up space. I know guys who are doing whatever on the side and make their money and that. I try to make them understand that of course you've got to pay for this and pay for that but you need to make music your sole thing. If you're the kind of person who is focused and you've got that fire and that burn you'll make a way in music. You'll find a way to get paid. If you're thinking about something else that is nothing to do with it, it takes as much mental space and time. It's conflicting. You're kind of fucking yourself up."

That Dylan Mills made it out of his predicament and succeeded to the extent that he did as Dizzee Rascal is nothing short of extraordinary, but then he was lucky when it came to father figures who would lend him a helping hand out of the mire. And after Danny Shittu and Tim Smith those male role models kept coming, just when Dizzee needed them most.

Another pivotal figure in his teens was Nick Cage (real name Nick Denton), who would become his manager and, later, co-owner of his Dirtee Stank record label, as well as his producer. Cage first stumbled upon Dizzee when the entrepreneur and producer was a 38-year-old self-proclaimed "fat old bastard", while the wannabe artist was a 16-year-old intent on gaining a foothold in London's emergent grime scene – as Cage later joked, around this time Dizzee was so keen to get started he would play not just local raves and concert shows but funerals and bar mitzvahs, too.

Apart from his production and engineering nous and his managerial skills, Cage had a fearsome reputation, the sort of character you didn't really want to get on the wrong side of. A few years after his and Dizzee's first meeting, just after the latter's notorious near-fatal stabbing in grime hotspot Ayia Napa, *Vice* magazine published a picture of Dizzee holding a knife; Cage's response was to threaten to tear the UK editor of the publication, Andy Capper, "limb from limb".

That first encounter was memorable for both parties. The 16-year-old Dizzee who came crashing into Cage's studio in 2001, as he laid down some tracks for a pioneering early grime single called 'Bounce', had the energy of a young man who was determined to make something of his life, but who was already saddled with a lot of anger from his childhood. As Cage told Tim Adams of *The Observer* in 2009, the young Dizzee Rascal "was certainly channelling aggression" on that fateful occasion, and was far from the confident twentysomething pop star that he is today. Cage remembers him as someone who was "baffled by things" and paints a vivid but sad picture of the teenager leaving behind the people in the studio to go and sit outside on a chemical waste bin behind the building, where he stayed for several hours in silent contemplation as the acid from the bins ate away at his jeans.

With the benefit of hindsight, Cage put Mills' troubled nature down to a lethal cocktail of confusion about his father's death, rage as a result of his subsequent upbringing as an only child in relative poverty on a dilapidated estate, and the powerful marijuana he had by then begun to smoke in considerable quantities. No wonder, he surmised, there were "no end of voices" in Dizzee's head, making the angry but intelligent young man feel alienated from the crowd.

"The thing about Dizzee was that he was living street life, but he was extremely clever," Cage told Adams. "And there is nothing worse than being clever or creative and having no outlet, or being in peer groups where people think you are weird if you want to work hard at something." Sensing that he was different from his peers, Cage immediately felt protective towards him, and tried to comfort him about his acid-ravaged trousers, but soon realised that his problems ran far deeper than that.

Although he was reluctant to indulge in too much exploration of Dizzee's complex make-up, or to delve too deeply into any cod-analysis of what might be seen as their father-son dynamic, Cage did admit to feeling paternal towards his soon-to-be-protégé, as he told Ben Thompson of *The Observer* in 2007. "There was some of that, yeah," he said. "Probably because no one else did. He was in bits, really. So I was chatting to him and alerted him to the fact that his jeans might rot. But then I realised that there were deeper issues than that, cos he was still sat there three hours later."

Dizzee was fortunate to find a manager as reliable and understanding as Cage, especially in a milieu as rife with tensions and backstabbing as London's nascent grime scene. He told music website UK Music that artists need to pick their manager as carefully as they do their record label or producer: it has to be someone they believe in, and who believes in them. "It should be someone you trust," he advised. "Don't be fooled by someone who looks the part, and says, 'I'm a manager.' Look into them."

If Dizzee was lucky to have met Cage, the rest of his journey was down to determination and sheer hard graft. Perhaps Dizzee Rascal's ultimate triumph was the way he channelled his negative energy and violent, antisocial tendencies, managed to defeat the demons in his head and turn it all towards the creation of radically original music. As he told Ed Marriot of *The Times*, "Even when I was getting kicked out of school I still made music. I found a way to channel my energies into being creative instead of destructive." He further explained that he was committed to doing whatever it took to avoid any of the things that could trigger a violent bust-up or any of the other sort of delinquent acts that characterised his early teenage years. "[I try] not to be around anyone long enough to have a disagreement and, if I do, I just walk away," he admitted. "I just try to let it go".

CHAPTER 3

Brand New Day

"The saviour of UK music has finally arrived and – gasp – he's not carrying a guitar, although he is armed with a fair share of teen angst."
Pitchfork reviewer

According to grime lore, it was actually MC and music producer Wiley who introduced Dizzee Rascal to Nick Cage after Dizzee came to Wiley's attention via his stints on pirate radio. Still, whoever it was, and however it happened, the connection between future star and producer was now made, and British rap would never be the same again.

Wiley's contribution to London's, and the UK's, music scene was also considerable. Born Richard Kylea Cowie in 1979, he was, like Dylan Mills, born in Bow, but being half a decade older than Dizzee, he became involved in the local scene far earlier – his earliest recordings are said to date back to 1998 (apparently involving him rapping over jungle beats on pirate radio), and although Dizzee himself made his first single only a couple of years later, that time differential, in a scene as head-spinningly fast-moving as the UK dance underground, counts for a lot. Wiley has since then assumed near-legendary status, and acquired a reputation for being contradictory, enigmatic and elusive. Above all, he is considered a prime mover in the evolution of British electronic dance music from jungle/drum'n'bass to garage and eventually to grime, of which he is regarded in many circles as the originator, along with Dizzee Rascal.

In fact, Wiley and Dizzee's stories became intertwined around the turn of the decade. The period 2000–1 saw Wiley join, form, dissolve and switch between garage crews – with names like the Ladies Hit Squad and Pay As U Go Cartel (a pioneering collective to rank alongside So Solid Crew who in 2002 had a Top 40 hit with 'Champagne Dance') – with alarming speed. Members of these crews would come and go, mainly due to disputes caused by the seemingly infinite number of micro-initiatives, with regard to the latest mad beats and intense urban sonics, that they each wanted to pursue.

And so the enterprising Wiley (who later could boast two clothing ranges and in 2008 reached number two with the 'Wearing My Rolex' single) decided to pull together an aggregate of MCs and DJs who would conform to his own personal vision of what the future direction of underground UK urban music should be. This was the Roll Deep super-collective, featuring more than a dozen of London's finest decks wizards and lyric spitters (some of them Dizzee's former schoolfriends), who would help speed up the process by which UK garage became that new strain of British hip hop known as grime (they would also be, at the time of writing this book, May 2010, number one in the UK singles chart with 'Good Times').

This startling new mutation was soon typified by its dizzyingly fast, complex breakbeats and darting, dolorous basslines, its assimilation of elements from drum'n'bass, rap and dancehall, and its futuristic sonics evocative of some near-off urban dystopia. It was a menacing, even chilling sound that Wiley would term "eski", short for "eskibeat", to suggest the often disconcertingly icy atmosphere of this music – Wiley himself even had instrumental titles such as 'Blizzard', 'Eskimo' and 'Ice Rink', using meteorological and environmental imagery to connote cold-heartedness and to conjure a bleak psychogeographic space that perfectly suited wintry inner London at night.

The intuitive Wiley was sufficiently discerning to realise that this young local boy called Dizzee Rascal, who had begun to acquire a reputation through pirate radio and seemed to share his musical vision, would function well in Roll Deep. And so he invited Dizzee to join the group (that other commercialising force from the grime underground, Tinchy Stryder, would also later become a member of the RD crew). "I'd been bothering Wiley for ages, man," recalled Dizzee in *The Observer*. "He just thought, 'Ah — little kid in the area.' He probably didn't take me serious, but you come to the point where you stop talking and just do."

It is unclear what happened next. At various points in the very early Noughties, Dizzee Rascal and Wiley recorded the tracks 'We Ain't Having It' and 'Mash Up' (which never saw an official release); Dizzee made some of his own brilliantly crude recordings including 'Wheel', 'Ho and Go' and 'Streetfighter' featuring him rapping over chopped-up beats and video-game sonics; and he collaborated with various other MCs and DJs, all before he wrote his first solo single proper, 'I Luv U', and signed to the major label, XL, that would bring him overground success. Also in this murky part of his story, he won a Sidewinder (a hardcore grime/rave night/event) award for Best Newcomer MC and formed a double-act with Wiley — their performance at Sidewinder is considered to be one of the pivotal moments in the development of grime. The pairing was short-lived: after Nick Cage secured a deal for Dizzee, Wiley, also managed by Cage, left him behind as he believed it was he that Cage should have been pushing. Wiley regretted not having Cage in charge of his career any longer; his reason for terminating their business relationship was, he said, jealousy that the manager "preferred Dizzee".

The truly seminal moment of record, and recorded moment, however, is widely regarded to be Roll Deep's track 'Bounce'. It was this tune from 2002, featuring the likes of Biggie Pitbull, Scratchy,

Breeze, Jet Le, Jamakabi, Bubbles, Flowdan and Wiley himself (who wrote it) that Nick Cage was recording a vocal hook for on that fateful day (see Chapter 2) in his studio in Deptford, south-east London, when Dizzee came skulking in. It occurred to Cage that this MC upstart would be ideal for the final version of 'Bounce', and so it was that, through a circuitous series of circumstances, Dizzee Rascal made his recorded début.

His vocal contributions to the track were striking: among the other MCs, with their deeper, gruffer, more traditionally manly tones, Dizzee's voice was so high it was as though it had barely broken; almost a squawk or yelp, a truly unusual instrument, capable of expressing rage and confusion, as well as conveying aggression and threat. But there was a playful edge to it, and a near-comical quality that was quite unique and suggested here was someone who would have a similarly askew world view.

When asked by *The Observer* a few years later what he made of this troubled but charismatic and cocksure youngster, producer Nick Cage replied: "He was awake, that's what I thought, cos I was around a lot of very sleepy people. Everyone's sitting there in a coma, and he gets more work done in 10 minutes than they did in two days. He comes in, does his verse. He's all over the mixing desk trying to find out how it works, and in terms of studio technique, he's a natural. So that was all good and impressive."

He also noted that, apart from his sense of discipline, determination and prodigious energy, Dizzee also had an enormous capacity for industrial-strength weed, which he had perhaps acquired partly in a bid to fit in with the others on the scene, many of whom were at least four or five years older than him. "Obviously," surmised Cage, "he's got to overcompensate for being young and being the whipping boy." So instead of recoiling from the powerful marijuana, which would have made him lose face, he would consume it with gusto. As Dizzee said, "So I went at it – it was a challenge."

The greatest challenge, however, was to cement his burgeoning reputation as an MC of note, both because it was the most obvious way for him to escape the life of crime that had at one point seemed inevitable, and because it was fast becoming evident he had much to say, both musically and lyrically. Dizzee began working at a furious rate, in the process demonstrating a fearlessness – in a milieu known for its intense competitiveness, its local rivalries and jealousies – that both intimidated and aggravated his peers. "I started getting better than people," he told journalist Ben Thompson. "Let's be real, that's what happened." But as Nick Cage pointed out, this tended to wind people up, some of whom expressed their ire in the most physical ways imaginable. "Guys would come and attack him with concrete posts and bricks," he recalled, adding that Dizzee would routinely refuse to back down, fearless of violent confrontations. "He would always face it out, take them all on." Cage remembered that, for the young MC, performing in a different area of London would be like running the gauntlet of alien gangs. "You'd be forever getting into some confrontation on the street. Four guys would come up. 'What are you doing here?' They would know Dizz was from the East End or whatever. Postcode wars, all that shit." Dizzee, ever self-deprecating, admitted that he wasn't always as courageous as some reports indicate: "Sometimes I had to twist and run as well," he has said.

Many of his problems were due to his catholic musical taste for everything from jungle to grunge – he even told Emma Warren of *Dummy* magazine in 2009 that, during lunchtimes at school, he would play in indie rock bands, in which he'd be the one "mucking about on drums or guitar". Then there was his steadfast refusal to kowtow to the underground's rules, just as he had once avoided the strictures of full-time education. Not everyone on east London's nascent grime scene had his breadth of vision, even as grime was coalescing as a bona fide distinct musical form, when it was "just a bunch of kids whose only avenues were pirate radio and the kind of raves that no journalists would ever go to". Back then, when grime was the next logical evolution from garage and drum'n'bass, it was just made "for all the kids who couldn't get into clubs, because they didn't have the suit and the shoes". Whereas garage was like a latter-day disco – music for upwardly mobile teens and twentysomethings who liked dressing up – grime was harsher, grittier, reflecting the world as it was rather than a varnished, romanticised version of the truth. "We were street boys – talking about what we knew," Dizzee said. This earned him criticism from the outset, detractors "bitching and moaning" that he lacked the right ghetto credentials and therefore didn't merit true "hood" status. His response was direct: "I don't have to answer to none of these dickheads," he said, claiming that his music wasn't designed to appease small-minded bigots. "Everything I do is for the music," he averred. "I want to master it like Bruce Lee mastered martial arts."

Dizzee has insisted that he has never needed to go into too much detail about this early phase of his career, simply because it was all there in the music: he used his songs to document his travails and record his observations on life as he experienced it. And there are few songs more vivid in their verisimilitude, nor more accurate in their account of modern street life, than 'I Luv U', the first song Dizzee Rascal ever wrote, which he penned when he was just 16 years old (it would later be the lead single from *Boy In Da Corner*).

It was an astonishing first foray. Lyrically, 'I Luv U' couldn't have been more full-on, a tumult of language that, even without the demented sonics, effectively created a sense of clamour and confusion. The words were noisily expressed, all street argot and freshly minted vernacular, with nods to Wiley's chilly "eski" sensibility in the allusions to wintry Russian cities and graphic references to sex that reduced love to a series of brutally brief, cold exchanges between barely consenting, mutually distrustful adolescents (it was probably news to those not from Dizzee's "hood" that "shines" was a synonym for oral gratification). From the girlie loop of "I love you" and Dizzee's immortal "yo" 40 seconds in to the part at the end, where Dizzee made the impudent but quite superfluous declaration (mainly because he'd spent the previous three minutes proving otherwise) of his rampant articulacy, 'I Luv U' didn't let up for an instant. It was like one of those True Romance cartoon

Dizzee in 2003: "Music was the only option open to me." (GEMMA BOOTH/CORBIS OUTLINE)

Dylan Kwabena Mills. (REX FEATURES)

The flat in east London where Dizzee grew up.
(REX FEATURES)

Langdon Park Secondary School, where Dizzee met teacher Tim Smith. (REX FEATURES)

Hoodie two shoes. (EVA EDSJO/REDFERNS)

Dizzee and Wiley in June 2003. Rolex not pictured. (DAVID TONGE/RETNA UK)

"I want to thank God, my mum and my family and everyone in the underground": Dizzee with his Mercury Music Prize, 2003. (REX FEATURES)

NME of the people: Dizzee holds his award for Innovation. (DAVE HOGAN/GETTY IMAGES)

Live and dangerous: performing at the Bristol Academy on November 2, 2004. (MATT CARDY/GETTY IMAGES)

Portrait of Dizzee Rascal in November 2003. (EDD WESTMACOTT/RETNAUK)

Bling of pop. (REX FEATURES)

Point blank. (ANDY PARADISE/REX FEATURES)

On *Last Call With Carson Daly.* (MICHAEL SIMON/REX FEATURES)

strip sagas that teenage girls used to read in magazines such as *Jackie*, only updated for the 21ˢᵗ century and rated 18. It presented a darkly comic picture of a pregnant teenage girl and concomitant teenage boy reluctant to fall prey to a life of commitment, with attendant references to the games manipulative females play and the techniques young men employ to avoid being trapped. As sharply observed vignettes of the capital's underclass went, it was miles apart from, but belonged in the same class as, such all-time inner-London classics as The Kinks' 'Waterloo Sunset', Squeeze's 'Up The Junction' and The Jam's 'Down In The Tube Station At Midnight'.

Then there was the manner in which this *vérité* tale was delivered. Half rap-speak and ragga chat, Dizzee sounded urgent, desperate for attention, in a perpetual state of panic, his verbal style superfast, staccato and spittle-flecked, at once deathly serious and cartoonishly frivolous, emphasising the all-too-real nature of the protagonist's predicament, torn between droll contempt and spite. Even without a soundtrack, 'I Luv U' would have been pure hubbub and hullabaloo. As Dizzee commented in 2002, "There is so much to care about in this world… If you give a shit, you'll go nuts." If this was any measure, Dizzee's head was dizzily busy, busting with things to say for fear that, if he didn't free them, it would burst.

Meanwhile, the music was almost science fictional in its angular futurism, and it didn't so much borrow from past genres (from rock to rave, rap to ragga) as chop and dice them up with psychotic finesse. It was produced by Dizzee and Nick Cage as though the latter were a distant, post-techno relation of avant-garde composer John Cage, and expressed that feeling of imminent meltdown alluded to by Rascal above ("You'll go nuts") with aplomb. It opened with some cymbal crashes and the cold, clinical whack of a metal beat, interspersed with a cut-up female vocal that robotically, repeatedly droned "I luv u". After that came a deluge of punkishly frenetic electronic noise, like Kraftwerk playing The Clash's 'White Riot', or sampladelic pioneers Art Of Noise chopping and dicing Sham 69's yob-punk anthem 'Borstal Breakout' into thrillingly strange new cubist shapes, full of startling stops and starts, random bursts of synthesized bass and glacial keyboards.

Not for nothing did rock critic Simon Reynolds compare Dizzee Rascal's first effort – self-issued as a white label ahead of a proper release the following year after his producer and manager, Cage, negotiated a deal for his charge with XL Records – to the seminal, seismic first detonation by The Sex Pistols, and declare that the artist was "the most impressive and provocative English MC since Tricky". Reynolds, who began his Blissblog site in the early Noughties in part to spread the word about Dizzee and the scene to which he belonged, wrote extensively and eulogistically about 'I Luv U'. He described the singer's wild, wired screech as "a voice like wounded eyes... strung taut between lashing-out and tears, its rapid-fire, blurting rhythm... like thoughts racing so fast they trip over themselves." That voice, he furthered, was "unique, quirky, but also collective, the sound of the streets", while Dizzee's back-story "told of the struggle of an exceptional individual but also someone who was the product of an environment". Concluded Reynolds of a track he saw as the next logical advance for urban street music: "'I Luv U' hits with the force of an aesthetic ambush: this ain't UK garage as we've known it... You know you're witnessing the birth of the New Thing. I want to believe this is the real-deal paradigm shift so much that I can't trust what my ears are telling me: that it is."

The highly influential Pitchfork music website was equally declamatory about 'I Luv U'. "It's about fucking time," wrote the reviewer. "The saviour of UK music has finally arrived and – gasp – he's not carrying a guitar, although he is armed with a fair share of teen angst." It went on to compare Dizzee with other garage and proto-grime artists, deciding that, compared to 'I Luv U', "So Solid Crew look like the wankstas they invariably are; Dizzee Rascal makes spittle-flecked inner city soundtracks more 'urban' than The Streets and Tim Westwood's usual playlist multiplied." It proceeded to praise "the most rudeboy super-XR3I speaker-fucking bassline" as well as its "fantastic attention to the detail of a typical bad boy conversing with his slaggy hoop-earring lass", concluding with a triumphant: "Single of the goddamn year."

In becoming Dizzee Rascal, and with this one track in particular, the 16-year-old Dylan Mills had turned his life around and changed his destiny from directionless petty hoodlum to one of the most exciting new voices to emerge in British music in decades.

CHAPTER 4

World Outside

"I think this country needs to listen to this country more. Americans speak English: what are US rappers gonna tell us in our own language? There's ghettos here – it's not recognised. We're underneath… And we're about to blow up and rise."

Dizzee Rascal

Not that everyone in the outside world – the world outside the grime underground – was immediately receptive to the startling new voice heard on 'I Luv U'. The first two groups of people to respond excitedly to Dizzee Rascal's début single were, naturally, pirate radio aficionados, and, perhaps less obviously, internet bloggers – it was, in fact, the latter who helped spread the word, virally, about this amazing new talent and bring him to wider attention.

'I Luv U' was first released during the summer of 2002 as a white label by a record company conceived by Dizzee and co-run with his manager/producer, Nick Cage. The pair decided to call it Dirtee Stank Recordings, the name, explained Dizzee, coming from one of his early lyrics. Dirtee Stank predated Dizzee's major label deal with

XL, who issued his first three albums, up to and including 2007's *Maths + English*. After the initial flurry of activity surrounding 'I Luv U', Dirtee Stank fell inactive until Dizzee 'revived' it in 2005 when he signed two acts – Klass A and Newham Generals.

On the label's MySpace page there is a statement about its *modus operandi* and ethos, presumably written by Dizzee: "The label is about bridging the gap between indies, majors and the street. Stank is the way forwards." It also explains why Dizzee chose the logo, which features some faeces hovered over by buzzing flies: "Because it was the dirtiest, gulliest think I could think of." In addition, Nick Cage has said that Dirtee Stank "exists to promote gifted artists with 'social problems' that might scare off other labels; people who, through the conditions they live in, might not be stable." The label, he continued, should also "help artists overcome hurdles such as access to studios that take something from a raw demo to something people will get excited about on the street." Cage could have been talking about Dizzee himself.

Street-level excitement is exactly what 'I Luv U' generated, and Dirtee Stank did a job every bit as effective as an indie, if not a major, with regard to capitalising on that buzz. After being played incessantly on pirate radio throughout summer 2002, 'I Luv U' became a huge underground hit and street anthem, its initial vinyl run selling out in days. It eventually shifted over 15,000 white label copies, which inevitably attracted the interest of bigger record companies and incited a bidding war.

The virtual community of internet music writers and commentators played no small part in the single's early success, engendering a sense of "intense blogospheric fervour", as influential rock and dance critic Simon Reynolds put it. The author of Blissblog (http://blissout.blogspot.com/), Reynolds – who is from the Home Counties and was for many years based in New York (he moved to LA in June 2010) – spent the summer of 2002 in London and first heard 'I Luv U' as a white label being heavily rotated on pirate radio, when it was available only in specialist record shops. It was the instrumental flipside version, whose "gabba-like bass blasts sounded like revolution", that initially caught his ear, but when the pirate DJs began playing the vocal version, that one, he said, "started to signify a revolution, too: one of those epoch-defining moments on a par with The Sex Pistols' 'Anarchy In The UK'".

At the time, nobody else – or at least, no one in the mainstream press – was writing about Dizzee Rascal and so he became a *cause célèbre* for music bloggers such as Reynolds. Soon, other bloggers in the UK, US and Australia followed his lead, having tracked down the MP3. After much file sharing, word about this new artist began to spread, and by the start of 2003, after Reynolds had made 'I Luv U' his Single of the Year on Blissblog, Dizzee was able to boast a ready-made, online network of fans in Britain and the States.

In an interview with *The Guardian* about the proliferation of new media and the new methods of disseminating information about music, Reynolds pointed out that "the communications network of choice for the music underground in which Dizzee Rascal operates is made up of pirate radio, mobile phones and SMS messages" – and blogs. "The blogs had a big role in building buzz on Dizzee outside the underground scene itself," he said. "Someone as talented as Dizzee would rise regardless. But I do think 'we' helped get things started in terms of the music media. I reckon a lot of music journalists check out the blogs." It had reached the point where record company executives were starting to take online tastemakers' opinions as seriously as those from the traditional print media. Speaking in the same article in *The Guardian*, *NME*'s then-editor, Conor McNicholas, opined that, although "blogs don't have an impact on mass market sales", someone like Dizzee's success was "partly down to word of mouth through the industry. And the industry certainly does take notice of dedicated fan sites."

Simon Wheeler, head of new media for the Beggars Group (which owns XL, the label to which Dizzee signed in the wake of the white label success of 'I Luv U'), agreed that the buzz surrounding Dizzee Rascal in the blogs and file-sharing networks gave them the confidence to take a punt on this audacious, idiosyncratic new artist. "It backed up our opinion that Dizzee was someone who would inspire a lot of people once they were exposed to him," he told *The Guardian*.

Dizzee knew that the time was right for a new type of British urban music that, for once, wasn't simply a localised take on American hip hop; one with its own distinctive flavour and language. As he said at the time, comparing and contrasting US rappers with the burgeoning grime scene's MCs: "I think this country needs to listen to this country more. Americans speak English: what are [US rappers] gonna tell us in our own language? There's ghettos here – it's not recognised. We're underneath… And we're about to blow up and rise."

'I Luv U' was voted one of the best songs released between 2000 and 2003 in the 2008 book *The Pitchfork 500: Our Guide To The Greatest Songs From Punk To The Present*. It unleashed a tsunami of praise and a desire to understand Dizzee, who was responsible, as UK Music put it, for "making ghetto life this season's new black". In an interview with the music website, he expressed his distrust of the majority of music industry insiders that he had met thus far – "It [the industry] is full of people who've got nothing to do with music, to be honest," he said – and admitted that he found it odd that he was suddenly being barraged with questions about himself from complete strangers (ie journalists), keen to know all about this extraordinary new act and his equally extraordinary new music. He admitted that he found his first interviews "nerve-racking", since he was unaccustomed to being either probed about his private life or asked to discuss issues that he had never really considered before. "When you've got a street attitude you can be kinda ignorant," he said, "so somebody might ask me a question and I'll be like, 'What?! I don't wanna answer that.' But it's about applying yourself." He revealed that, among other things, he was inspired by "life in general – I like girls, money…" And he acknowledged the responsibilities that came with his new role as figurehead for the youth. "I try and say some positive things for the young but I'm not a role model," he said. "I like to think of myself more as an inspiration for kids to carry on what they're doing."

Dizzee may have been feeling the pressure, with the heat of the spotlight being trained on him by the media – but this was before 'I Luv U' had even seen an official release by a 'proper' record company. When he finally did ink a deal with XL in early 2003, the expectation was that the single, rerecorded and re-produced by Jacob Freitt, and given a full-blown rerelease, would storm to the top of the charts. If it did indeed achieve crossover success, it wouldn't have been the first grime hit – as Simon Reynolds has pointed out, "grime – before it existed as a term or even a separate genre, when it was MCs rapping over 2-step garage beats – actually started at the top of the charts, in the form of number one hits for Oxide & Neutrino's 'Bound 4 Da Reload' [in May 2000] and So Solid Crew's '21 Seconds' [in August 2001]". But 'I Luv U' was grime as "a distinct sonic entity", and there had yet to be a bona fide grime crossover – or "crash-over", as Reynolds put it, given the music's sheer heft and harsh, angular sound – smash. Perhaps not surprisingly, then, when it was reissued in May 2003, any hopes that it would 'do' a 'Smells Like Teen Spirit' or 'God Save The Queen', scale the upper echelons of the charts and subvert a nation, were dashed when it only reached number 29 – "no doubt," opined Reynolds, "too disruptive for radio".

It could have been its storyline that made it "too much" for daytime radio. This was, after all, a song about teenage pregnancy, and callous males and manipulative females fighting a verbal battle for supremacy. It detailed a relationship – more like a tense non-alliance – where sex is a weapon used to cudgel both parties in a social cul-de-sac, while the part where the male protagonist starts fantasising about a girl from college made it seem like an X-rated version of Pulp's 'Common People'. As for the references to oral sex and colourful language throughout ("whore", "bitch", etc), they necessitated a "clean radio edit", although clearly it wasn't clean enough; maybe it was all just too vivid and 'real' for mainstream consumption.

Or perhaps the language was too esoteric in its vernacular strangeness, Dizzee's comic rage just too idiosyncratically expressed.

Shortly after the single charted, an article appeared in *The Guardian* about this almost alien language that grime artists such as Dizzee Rascal, and young people in general, had begun to use on the street. Under the title 'Bow's Message to Blair', journalist Martin Clark wondered whether Dizzee's problem with regard to infiltrating the mainstream was a simple matter of (non-)comprehension. "The street language of Dizzee and his peers evolves daily," he wrote. "'Coch' means to move undetected; you don't say 'the street' but 'road'; a 'sket' is a sexually derogatory term for a girl; 'shotters' and 'blotters' are drug dealers; a 'screwface' is the scowl etched on inner-city faces. And we'll leave it to the Radio 1 playlist team to explain what a 'bowcat' is. Even a traditional word like 'real' gets reinvented. When things are getting 'real', life is harsh or violent."

But then, this was just Dizzee Rascal telling it like he saw it, using language that was all too familiar to him. This wasn't an attempt to obfuscate; he was simply being conversational. When Nick Hasted of *The Independent* met him around this time, the journalist was surprised to find a "small and calm" boy, with a "teenager's way of talking in jerky bursts", and "clear, interested eyes". Dizzee took the opportunity to talk about the London that he would detail so richly and powerfully on his then-imminent début album, *Boy In Da Corner*, the daily boredom and banality of his existence, the perennial tension that he felt around him and the occasional eruptions of violence – all the things that made him the explosively original talent that he was.

"I'd be out sitting on the wall all day," he reminisced. "Chat shit. Watch cars go past. Or do other stuff. I used to bottle things up, then explode, at the wrong time. Growing up on a council estate, that didn't really stand out. There's thousands of me. But eventually you have to be a rock, and stand firm and do your deal. Music was the first thing that channelled my energies. Where normally I'd be on the street starting trouble, I'd be in the studio, for hours. It was hard, at the beginning. But when I think about it now, it kept me out of so much – that fight, and that shooting."

He spoke about the music that he grew up with and absorbed almost from birth, from rappers such as Tupac Shakur and Eminem to London's junglist renegades to, more surprisingly, purveyors of punk, metal and grunge – which he termed "the extreme musics" – from Sham 69 to Nirvana. All of these would, he explained, eventually seep, by osmosis, into the grooves of *Boy In Da Corner*. He was particularly keen to talk about Nirvana's *In Utero*, the last record made by Kurt Cobain before his suicide in 1994, and an album that, like his own forthcoming début, had a sort of cathartic energy and purgative power.

"If you're feeling bad, it cleanses you, because the rage is in the music," he said. "So once the album's done, the anger's gone with it. It's been angry for you. I'd like people to think of my record from that point of view. A lot of people feel like me in this city. So they can turn it on for 60 minutes. And then, get on with things."

Finally, he agreed with journalist Hasted that it was the very harshness of his existence that made him someone that would appeal to middle-class listeners from cosy suburbia, and that gave him the strength and determination to make the music that he did – without that, he wouldn't be half the artist that he was.

"Yeah, of course," he said. "Street's with you forever. It's good, if you apply it to something else. It don't do much for you otherwise. I might never be socially accepted, or middle class. But you make your own straps when you're from the road. I ain't got nothing against middle- or upper-class people. I just ain't got much in common with them. I think it's more important to come from nothing and make yourself big." He paused, then said with a polite chuckle: "No disrespect to anyone born with a silver spoon in their mouth."

CHAPTER 5

Showtime

"Boy In Da Corner is one of the most assured début albums of the last five years."

Louis Pattison, *NME*

As 2003 progressed, it was becoming increasingly evident, at least for Dizzee Rascal, that "coming from nothing" was an absolute advantage in life. It was if *Boy In Da Corner* was any measure. As first forays go, it was truly mind-boggling, all the more so considering his age when he made it. A read through of the credits reveals that recording (at Raskits Lair/Belly Of The Beast Studios in London) took place between October 2001, when he would have just turned 16, and March 2003, when he was still only 17. He was still only 17 when the album was released in July 2003. Further scrutiny of the rear of the album sleeve shows that Dizzee wrote and produced the whole thing, with some production assistance on the odd track from his producer and manager, Nick Cage, and other names such as Chubby Dread, and Taz & Vanguard. There were also vocal contributions from, among others, Wiley (of whom he wrote on the sleeve foldout, "I love you like a brother – only blood separates us – fuck da bullshit, we roll deep", ironically just before their very public falling out – see Chapter Six) and Jeanine Jacques, who took the acridly pretty female lead part on the 'I Luv U' single, which also featured here.

But apart from that, this was Dizzee's show, all 15 tracks and 57 minutes of it; a startling display of solipsistic studio adventurism. Of course, it would have been astonishing had he been 20 or 25, but given that he was in his mid-teens when he wrote and produced this music, it made the achievement all the more impressive. *Boy In Da Corner* was just under an hour of furious musical invention and dazzling, witty, withering wordplay, as though Elvis Costello at his angriest had been reborn as a 17-year-old east London grime kid. If one ever wondered what exactly Dizzee got up to in Tim Smith's music room at Langdon Park Secondary School, here was the evidence – and it was ferocious in its radical futurism, an awesomely ambitious break with musical convention, with only the most tenuous connection to UK garage and US hip hop mores and practices. Here were processed metal guitars, disturbingly deployed found sounds, samples from a dizzying array of sources, bursts of noise that evoked the cacophony of inner London's streets as well as the computer game bleeps that emanate from indoors, all vying for space in the mix with glacial synth lines and the disconcertingly pretty tones of Japanese court music.

The prevalent rhythm – or anti-rhythm, considering how undanceable it was – on *Boy In Da Corner* was, according to one periodical, "a high-octane tribal skank", while the disorienting effect of all the sound bursts and low-flying sonic detritus was heightened by Dizzee's staccato, Sten-gun verbal attack, not so much a fusion as a frictional assembly of garage MC, rap, grime and ragga vocal styles. Images and ideas flew out of Dizzee's mouth with such frenetic force it was like being shouted, or squawked and sobbed, into submission.

In contrast to the laconic style of most garage MCs, Mills rhymed in a startling, panicked yelp. "I always ended up shouting and screaming," he said. "When you're on pirate radio, when the speakers are blaring and everything's loud and in your face, you have to shout. I just didn't sound good over garage. I had to produce my own beats, because I didn't really fit."

And not all of it was familiar; often it was as alien as a foreign tongue, or some strange new language. Some of the speech and subject matter were recognisable: a litany of alienated-youth plaints about broken families, faithless women, gun crime and under-siege male boasts. But Dizzee's lyrics saw a departure from standard rap braggadocio and 'bling' boasting, portraying him as a by turns vengeful and sensitive bystander who, instead of privileging riches and success, offered an unflinching, bleak view of life in council estate Britain, one full of random violence and crime, poverty, drug-dealing and underage pregnancy. Instead of tough-guy posturing, here was a sad, often suicidal young man driven to despair by the madness and misery that surrounded him.

Alexis Petridis of *The Guardian* was typically stunned by what he heard, by the overall impact of the music and the lyrics: "What emerged from Langdon Park's music room may well be the most original sound heard in British music for the best part of a decade," he wrote. "A thrilling, propulsive racket, Mills' take on garage features clattering, arrhythmic beats, screeching electronics and occasional bursts of rock guitar, the latter apparently the result of an unlikely love of Nirvana."

Across the pond, the response to *Boy In Da Corner* ("The title," he said, "is about my life at that time. I'd been that kid in the corner of the classroom, the street corner. I had my back against the wall in general") was equally rapturous, quite surprising considering how defiantly British this music, with its attendant references to local culture, was. US Journalist Jeff Chang, in an article in New York's prestigious *Village Voice* entitled 'Future Shock', saw it as a way forward. He had a romantic vision of the futuristic Dizzee, "kotched up in the flat, punching out riddims into cheap PC software, beats born of ringtones, video games, and staticky pirate-radio sounds". Chang even invoked American-Canadian sci-fi cyberpunk author William Gibson, talking of Dizzee's Gibson-esque "mirror-world" in which "patterns [are] de/recontextualized at the edge of recognition and seen in syrupy slo-mo." Heard in this way, the beats on *Boy In Da Corner* "quiver and throb, struggle for internal equilibrium, and often refuse to groove".

This was a long way from traditional dance music, even the more extreme variety emanating at the turn of the decade from UK clubs. It required a new type of dance to match Dizzee's new form of dance music. Fortunately, there was so much going on in these tracks, so much detail, that *Boy In Da Corner* functioned just as effectively as bedroom music or headphone music. It was almost too relentless in its rhythmic and verbal assault to respond to in any other way than still, startled contemplation. From start to finish, it refused to let up.

The album opener was 'Sittin' Here'. It set the radical tone, presenting as it did an as yet unheard, unclassifiable music that sounded like nothing before or since. It offered the impression that *Boy In Da Corner* would be a work where all pop – or rock, or rap, or jungle, or grime – rules would be either ignored or wholly discarded. An unfamiliar instrument (possibly a Japanese koto) was gently plucked against an irregular whip-cracking drum beat, like the sizzle of an electrical cable. The lyric was as shockingly unusual as the sounds, portraying a despondent, depressed Dizzee sitting at home, playing CDs and staring into space, numb from hours of late-night computer gaming, reminiscing about the relatively carefree days of his youth when he would play football in the sunshine and chat up the fresh-faced local girls. By contrast, the present saw him hassled by the police and his peers, wondering which way to turn, who if anyone he could trust and asking of himself, "Wahgwan", a Jamaican colloquialism for "what's going on?" It might not be too far-fetched, indeed, to see *Boy In Da Corner* as a 21st century Britgrime version of Marvin Gaye's 1971 album, *What's Going On*, another landmark collection that expressed the confusion, rage and paranoid disquiet of a young black musician.

Track two was 'Stop Dat' (backing vocals by Armour of Nasty Crew) and immediately provided comic relief after the bleak album opener, Dizzee name-dropping cartoon characters (Top Cat, Fred Flintstone) as he introduced listeners to the "screwface" – a grime phrase for a look of utter disdain – and asserted his eminence as an MC and a lothario (comparing his prowess in this area to Tom Jones). The character here couldn't have been more at odds with the sorrowful protagonist of 'Sittin' Here'. 'I Luv U' was next, and even in the context of the album, despite the stellar company, it still sounded amazing. 'Brand New Day' was another track that showed just how far off the beat(en) track Dizzee was prepared to wander, displaying the full range of his influences, reminiscent as it was of nothing so much as Japan's 1982 avant-pop hit 'Ghosts', the Far Eastern melody contrasting vividly with the guntalk and the general hostility that he witnessed on his estate.

'2 Far' featured Wiley and saw Dizzee cock a snook at cosy domesticity and romantic convention, as well as giving authority, particularly the British constabulary, the finger as he critiqued social division, pointing out the disparity between the haves and the have-nots. The music saw him strike a similarly defiant pose, as rhythmically jerky and nervy as UK garage or the avant-R&B of American producer Timbaland.

One listen to 'Fix Up, Look Sharp' and you could tell immediately that it would be the next single released from *Boy In Da Corner*. Again, it essayed a new type of music – not rock, not grime, not even a hybrid, but a combustible combination of the two. It featured a vocal sample of what sounded like Led Zeppelin's Robert Plant's infamous holler but was actually from a track called 'The Big Beat' by US rocker Billy Squier. The beat was massive, and hit with clinical precision, but what was striking about 'Fix Up...' was the way the beats were surrounded by space, allowing the wryly humorous brags and boasts to be heard (at one point, Dizzee rhymes "loo" with "crew" before referencing a budget local supermarket chain). 'Cut 'Em Off' was weird even by the standards of this album: it was slow, arrhythmic and stark, like industrial metal reduced to 18rpm and produced by David Sylvian – there was in fact a Japanese keyboard motif throughout. The song was also downright funny, referencing his low-hanging trousers to comically bathetic effect and displaying a cartoonishly surgical approach to violence.

'Hold Ya Mouf' featured rapper God's Gift, the latter's low growl, redolent of US rapper DMX's gruff bark, at the opposite end of the vocal spectrum to Dizzee's hysterical sob-squawk. The music was, once again, just about as experimental as mainstream pop has ever got; a hard-to-pigeonhole sort of futuristic pop music from a chart where the credo is, the further out and the less deliberately commercial, the better. And yet for all that, the music was as insidiously addictive as the most contrived bubblegum pop. The song also included probably the album's most notorious line about Dizzee being a problem for Anthony Blair.

"I didn't set out to challenge the system," he said. "[That line] was really blown up in the media. I didn't consciously think, 'Yeah, Tony Blair. I'm going to cause you trouble.' It was just something that came out when I was rapping. I do what's good for me. Like any artist, I'm just expressing how I feel."

'Round We Go' presented Dizzee the cynic, bemoaning the grimly cyclical nature of existence and taking a dim view of romance, with its graphic depictions of cold couplings, brutal sex and more of his Wiley-style callousness and disregard for emotion. Accusations that Dizzee was an equal opportunities misogynist leching after girls of all races and creeds, shapes and sizes. This was balanced out by the realisation that the girls in his songs were as selfish, unfaithful and heartless as the men. 'Jus' A Rascal' (featuring rapper Taz) was notable for Dizzee's rapid-fire delivery, which sounded scattershot but was actually clinically precise, every bon mot crucial to the portrait of the titular bad boy and his antisocial antics. A torrent of self-mythologising slanguage, this was as fast as Dizzee rapped on the album, making him sound like a ragga chatter on speed as he strived to squeeze in every one of the 600-plus words. It was also the closest he came to an approximation of traditional US bragspeak, but even so it was given a distinctly British inflection, a London flava. The idea expressed in 'Wot U On?' (additional vocals courtesy Caramel), that money is a more powerful force than love, was as old as the hills, but it seemed fresh given the musical context, all gunshot beats and sci-fi thriller synths, while the disquieting neologisms ("skitz", "scopse") and bewildering phraseology ("getting up your gums") made the track as exciting and new as everything else on *Boy In Da Corner*.

'Jezebel' had plucked pizzicato strings throughout, a reminder of this music's roots in, yet simultaneous distance from, the garage scene that birthed it. It was alien yet accessible, a difficult trick to pull off, yet one that Dizzee managed superbly on *Boy In Da Corner*. The prettiness of this track's music – and it really was incredibly pretty – was entirely at odds with the dismal account of an underage mother destined for sexual disease and penury and the cycle of inner-city deprivation and despair. The frenetic sonics of 'Seems 2 Be' (additional vocals by Claire Cottrell) made evident Dizzee's astonishing facility with the studio and confidence to pursue whatever direction took his fancy. The lyric was an ambivalent observation of the street hustler's life interspersed with comical shout-outs to his aunt Maureen and his mum as she caught him smoking weed, the humorous asides proving there was room for laughter amid the gloom and the local references enhancing the quintessentially London ambience. 'Live O' was an audacious assembly of sonar bleeps and synth burps, with a rhythm that challenged even the most agile terpsichorean to move in time. Again, the radical future-shock quality of the music was at odds with the quaintly British references (to croquet), the allusions to Fifties pop (the song "I've Got To Wash That Man Right Out Of My Hair" from the musical *South Pacific* bizarrely gets a mention) and the arcane boasts (there's a shout-out to ancient Greek philosopher Aristotle) in this, another tune that cast women in a bad light, as untrustworthy and just plain worthy of contempt – Dizzee's sexual politics and attitude to women were perhaps the only elements of the album that were hard to admire.

'Do It!' featured another Oriental-style keyboard pattern, strikingly deployed and impressively pretty given the milieu. The track was remarkable for Dizzee's use of space, allowing the synth motif to breathe, taking the listener out of (t)his world, a world of urban deprivation and gangs. Most remarkable of all were the poignant lyrics in which Dizzee admitted that, overwhelmed by the daily struggle and grind, he was sometimes seized with a desire to end it all and enter an endless sleep. 'Do It!' couldn't have been a more fitting closer to *Boy In Da Corner*, a breathtaking final stop on this *tour de force* of an album (there was a bonus track called 'Vexed' tacked on to the end of the US edition). But the dolorous tone of 'Do It!' didn't tell the whole story, nor did the antagonistic nature of Dizzee's sleeve credits ("To all my haters, enemies and those who didn't believe I could [would] make it... Fuck you!!!").

There was, however, a more uplifting note on the sleeve, a touching acknowledgment of his former teacher from Langdon Park, who had subsequently left for another school: "Special thanx to Mr Smith, da best teacher Langdon Park ever let go (you fools). I'll never forget da way you kept your faith in me, even when things looked grim".

Dizzee explained why he credited his former teacher, saying, "Obviously Tim Smith has played a big part in my success, and the album was written to reflect how I felt and much of it came from my school days. I had to credit Mr Smith on the CD. I was never going to forget him. I'm not like that." Smith himself was understandably overjoyed at being immortalised on the sleeve of such a brilliant album. "I was thrilled to find out that he had credited me on his album," he said, admitting that he was sceptical at first, assuming it was just a wind-up. "A journalist phoned me before I heard the album. He told me what Dizzee had written. I said, 'Come on, get real.' He said, 'No, it's on the album.' 'Well, that's fantastic,' I said. I was really chuffed. It's my job to help all the students, but Dylan has done particularly well. I'm very proud of him, and it's nice to be remembered." He continued: "I've been a teacher for 26 years and I've seen other talented students come and go but never achieve this kind of success. It's also got me a lot of cred at my new school. One of his tunes came on the radio recently and a lad was miming all the words, so I asked him if he liked Dizzee Rascal. He asked me how I knew him, so I told him that I used to teach him at Langdon Park. Instant cred."

The front cover of *Boy In Da Corner* oozed cred, the street variety. It showed Dizzee, a hooded figure in stark black and white against the bright yellow walls of what looked like a padded room, making devil signs with his fingers over his head, apparently beleaguered and backed, seated, his body sunken and his legs outstretched, into the titular corner. But the truth was that *Boy In Da Corner* couldn't have been more of a triumph for the boy from Bow.

Reviewers were almost unanimous in their praise, on both sides of the Atlantic. In the *NME*, Louis Pattison pointed out the paradox presented by a music being hailed as "the future" whose essential message was "there is No Future" and that appeared to be providing the soundtrack to the impending apocalypse. "[*Boy In Da Corner*] sounds like balaclava-clad gangs of teenagers wiring London's tenement blocks with dynamite and razing them to the ground," he wrote, concluding that it was "one of the most assured début albums of the last five years". *The Guardian* paid tribute to "the churning bass frequencies, disturbing choruses of muttering voices, clattering synthesisers that recall police sirens and arcade games, and, on forthcoming single 'Fix Up, Look Sharp', bursts of rock guitar" and decided that to ignore Dizzee Rascal would be to disregard "the most original and exciting artist to emerge from dance music in a decade".

Over in the States, *Blender* hailed its "chaos of shrill synthetic sounds, distorted bass and beats that don't just stutter – like Dizzee himself, they tic and burst as though they've got Tourette's", while his delivery, they claimed, made him sound utterly alien. "He's only an ocean away, but this kid sounds like an extraterrestrial." *Entertainment Weekly* was in thrall to the "homemade beats and clammy, trapped-in-the-Underground ambience", the "knob-twirling sound effects and skittish, booming bass lines punctuated by firecracker bursts, answering-machine beeps, and electronic whiplashes", and decided that the songs constituted "one of the strangest, bumpiest musical journeys we're likely to experience on record this year".

The magazine did counter the praise by declaring that, "At its most tedious, the CD sounds like a caffeinated voice nattering on over videogame blurts and beeps" and was ambivalent about the claustrophobic unease produced by "the all-encompassing anxiety" and "amelodic minimalism" that dominated the album. US website Pitchfork was, however, utterly unequivocal. "Dizzee Rascal instantly stakes a claim that east London is hip hop's next great international outpost," the site said, comparing his tortured rapper persona to that of the ill-fated Tupac Shakur. "His rhymes, and especially his beats, reflect his area's desperate social, economic and political landscape... To wunderkind Rascal, the accelerated disintegration of his immediate world pains him – absolutely wounds him – and it's the Tupac-esque mix of brio and vulnerability, along with his dexterous cadence and gutter beats, that separates his rhymes from the typical money/cash/hoes triptych." The album's beauty, they decided, lay in its very ugliness and determination to match the brutality of Dizzee's east London locale with "an icy orchestra of scavenger sounds", the perfectly imperfect context for what they described as Dizzee's "unravelling psyche". Most critical of all was the connection the website reviewer made between Dizzee's "despairing wail, focused anger, and cutting sonics" and his angry/anguished young forebears: Johnny Rotten, Pete Townshend and Morrissey, drawing parallels between the "No Future" credo of The Sex Pistols' 'Anarchy In The UK', the "hope I die before I get old" pronouncement from The Who's 'My Generation', the allusion to suicide on The Smiths' 'Asleep' and Dizzee's own desire for oblivion on 'Do It!'. They concluded: "If Rascal grows at a similar rate, it's not out of the question that he could leave a comparable legacy."

It may have only entered the charts at number 40 and peaked at number 23 in the UK, but it sold over 58,000 copies in the States (where it was released by Matador) and over 250,000 copies worldwide, including more than 100,000 in the UK, where it earned a gold disc. It would win some of the most coveted awards in the music industry and eventually assume classic status, MTV Base voting it the sixth greatest album of all time in 2009. It also marked the start of the journey for Dizzee Rascal towards household name status.

However, as we shall see in the next chapter, Dizzee hadn't quite become a clean-cut mainstream pop star and escaped the scene that had, for the past few years, threatened to drag him deep into the mire. You couldn't yet say he was less cursed than blessed.

CHAPTER 6

Holiday In The Sun

"It's not glamorous. It was a bad time. I had internal bleeding in my chest so I was coughing up blood all the time. I was on a drip that was getting on my nerves. But I didn't want to make a meal of getting stabbed."

Dizzee Rascal

In the summer of 2003, Dizzee Rascal went to Ayia Napa, the holiday resort at the far eastern end of the south coast of Cyprus. It was his first visit to the Mediterranean island that had become the destination of choice for lovers of UK grime and garage, in much the same way that Ibiza had been the party capital for a previous generation of house, rave and techno clubbers. He was there to perform with the 13-strong garage collective Roll Deep Crew and to enjoy some time off after putting the finishing touches to his début album.

It was a memorable holiday for all the wrong reasons. Just as *Boy In Da Corner* was being released to widespread critical acclaim, on the evening of Monday July 7, Dizzee was attacked by a group of unknown youths. He was stabbed three or four, maybe even five or six times (depending on which account you believed), in the chest, back and buttocks. Reports also vary as to how and where it happened – some say it occurred outside a nightclub, others that he was attacked and stabbed by two men as he was riding his scooter, while a third report had it that he was pulled off the moped by four attackers armed with knives.

As to the reason for the attack, nobody knew that for sure, either. According to some, it was payback, but for what is not clear. Many of the British tabloids, reporting on the incident, suggested that it was connected to an apparent feud between Dizzee and controversial garage act So Solid Crew, who had a history linking them to criminal behaviour – member Jason Phillips, aka G-Man, for example, had just been jailed for four years after being found guilty of possessing a loaded handgun. Some said it may have been caused by Dizzee allegedly pinching or slapping the backside of SSC's Lisa (Finch) Maffia. Police spokesman Steve Theodoulou simply stated that the stabbing came a few hours after members of "two British music groups working in Ayia Napa were involved in a brawl".

The emerging grime star was rushed to hospital where he underwent an operation. A spokesman for the hospital said that he was "in a stable condition" and that he was "expected to leave hospital in the coming days" – he was released following treatment. In the aftermath of the event, another So Solid Crew member, Megaman – real name Dwayne Vincent – was questioned in connection with the stabbing, but was immediately released by Cypriot police. A statement issued by So Solid's publicist said: "Megaman has fully cooperated with the police, who have now eliminated him from their inquiries following the interview."

It was his manager, Nick Cage, who rushed to rescue Dizzee and resolve this grievous situation: he flew to Ayia Napa, nursed him, and then brought him back to England. In an interview with Tim Adams of *The Observer*, Cage revealed that he had to "nurse him for a fortnight in this manky hotel – the doctors were not nice to us, they refused to treat him. He looked like ET lying in the river. He had lost a hell of a lot of blood, and the wounds were in key places.

Major organs. It wasn't a casual slashing. He had checked himself out of hospital when I got there. He was high on painkillers, riding around on his moped, being pursued by tabloid journalists. I was like: wait until the painkillers wear off. I have lost three friends in these kinds of incidents – knifings. He was lucky."

If the stabbing drew Dizzee and Cage closer together, it effectively destroyed his friendship with Wiley. According to Wiley, Dizzee began to blame him for the situation (on his track 'Hype Talk', from his second album, *Showtime*, Dizzee claimed that Wiley just left him to rot in hospital, far from home). From this point onwards Cage would make it his life's work to protect Dizzee from trouble by keeping him out of harm's way – it was Cage who hid him away as soon as he came out of hospital, in order that he might avoid any recriminations and scurrilous gossip resulting from disputes that could have arisen with rival London crews.

And yet, while Cage felt that his charge needed protecting from others, some believed that the bad boy of grime really needed protecting from himself, such was his tendency to get into scrapes. Either way, Cage had become more than a manager and a mentor. He was now his saviour.

"Nick took me in as a kid," Dizzee said. "He could see that I was willing to go all out. So he went all out for me. We are family. We are from pretty much the same place... And he came and got me in Ayia Napa."

In an interview with US magazine *Blender*, Dizzee discussed the terrible incident in which he could so easily have lost his life. According to the now-defunct music monthly, Ayia Napa was a place where "anything goes", a place where street-tough Londoners went ostensibly to escape petty rivalries and find release from simmering local tensions but where, ironically, stoked by the drinking and late nights, "antagonisms between crews from different territories, held in check at home, boil[ed] over in the heat". Dizzee told *Blender* that, on that fateful night, he was set upon by members of So Solid Crew and that a fight occurred between him and So Solid's Megaman, which Dizzee claimed to have won. He was bloody but unbowed. "I'm not scared," he said. "If anything, I feel stronger." He wanted people to know the truth. "I punched up Megaman; I humiliated that boy," he said. "And every real nigga on the island knows what happened."

Following the stabbing, Dizzee was kept under police protection and Megaman was questioned, then released. Police announced that they were looking for two members of Cream Cartel, a crew affiliated with So Solid, who left the island shortly after Dizzee was stabbed. Thereafter, Dizzee was hospitalised, although it never occurred to him that he could have died. He just sat on his hospital bed threatening to get revenge and muttering "bastards" over and over. The night of the attack, Dizzee was racked by coughing fits, and as a result struggled to fall asleep. It was only in the morning that he realised it was blood from the wound on his chest that he had been coughing up. "I felt I'd been caught up in some madness," he explained. The Cypriot police, angry about what they saw as violence on their watch, proceeded to interrogate Dizzee, but he denied Megaman's involvement because he saw it as his responsibility to sort out, and no one else's, least of all the authorities. "I got a problem," he said, "I'm not going to the police."

Perhaps for shock value, or simply in the interests of factual reportage, *Blender*'s photographer wanted to shoot Dizzee for the article with his shirt off, which would have revealed the stab wound on his chest – a hole ringed by a bunch of stitch scars. But the star was uneasy about being presented as a sort of British counterpart to infamous US rapper 50 Cent, who had famously been shot several times and had the bullet wounds on his body to prove it. He wasn't sure whether he wanted the 'gangsta' appendage or any of the notoriety that went with it.

"I admire him," he said of the rapper sometimes known as Fiddy, "but to tell the truth, when I made my album, I would've gladly stayed behind the music as a producer. Coming out and being at the front is a lot to live up to."

Despite the bad feelings towards Wiley, Dizzee was keen to avoid laying the blame for the stabbing on anyone else. In fact, as he told *The Daily Star* some years later, he was partly to blame himself because he refused point blank to back down. "It was all in slow motion," he recalled. "I got off my bike doing the bravery thing when I should have just sped off, but I don't like to walk away. I don't like to be picked on. Growing up where I did you learn to fight." He added: "Getting stabbed, it's not glamorous. It was a bad time. I had internal bleeding in my chest so I was coughing up blood all the time. I was on a drip that was getting on my nerves. [But] I didn't want to make a meal of getting stabbed. And 50 Cent had already done it. I didn't want to compete with getting shot nine times."

Two months later, in September 2003, Dizzee was interviewed back in Britain by *The Guardian* newspaper, and he was still, understandably, guarded about Ayia Napa, and tried to dismiss the incident, simply saying that it was "a bit much".

"I did just take it like every other thing that's happened to me," he told Alexis Petridis. "I've been through madnesses before, violence. You can't say you're from the street and talk shit if you haven't been through those kind of experiences. I know that was a big thing, but I've been through stuff. When you do whatever stuff you do when you're from the street, you know what kind of thing can happen to you. When it happens to you, there's obviously a bit of shock and that, but you get over it, because you knew in the beginning that this could happen."

His response to the attack veered between nonchalance and honest admissions of disbelief that such a near-calamity could have occurred. In an interview with *X-Ray* magazine, he told journalist Lulu Le Vay that the stabbing had left him feeling more than a little shaken. "It was a shock, yeah," he said, "but to be honest it's just one of those things that happen. I was out and about a couple of days after the stabbing, but I think that was the drugs, innit! My adrenaline was up! I was stabbed five times, y'know?"

Mostly, though – either from a sort of perverse pride, self-protection, laddish bravado, or simply because he'd experienced other dramatic events in his short life – he brushed it off. "I've had other close shaves before; there's been some madness, y'know? I've been in three car crashes – one car blew up. Now that was a lot more scary than being stabbed up. I'm not going to dwell on it, not going to let it ruin my life." He listed some of his other injuries for the benefit of the *X-Ray* writer. "I broke my toe when I was younger, falling off a skateboard." He added: "The one thing you learn from living on the streets is how to hustle. Street hustle is all about coping with whatever environment you're in. This I can handle."

According to Dizzee, the ongoing row with So Solid Crew was based around a contretemps, not with Megaman, but another member, rapper and sometime actor Ashley Walters, alias Asher D, who had once challenged Dizzee to a rap contest. More seriously, he had been implicated in the gun controversies that surrounded So Solid Crew (following an argument with a traffic warden in July 2001, Walters was found to be carrying a loaded air pistol and, as a result, was arrested and subsequently jailed).

Although the impression given was that the Ayia Napa affair was the logical but dreadful corollary of the complex and potentially explosive rivalries within the UK garage scene, as far as Dizzee was concerned the stabbing incident was the result of a quite specific dispute, and in this instance he was at pains to absolve himself of responsibility. "Asher D dissed me first," he told Alexis Petridis of *The Guardian*. "I would never call somebody out for no reason. It's not in my nature. He [Asher D] came out of prison and he started talking." He insisted that, out of the whole garage scene, he was the one who kept himself to himself. "I've always been one to do my own thing. They can have their little wars and that, MCs clashing, whatever." He acknowledged, however, that people did indeed treat the internecine rivalries with life-or-death seriousness. "People take things very personally sometimes, because they've got that street mentality. People's egos, man: they'll fight about anything – they just happen to be doing music, you know? Everyone thinks they own the garage scene. I came into the garage scene altogether different. I've never been the same. But I don't care. Maybe it has made people more resentful of me, but whenever they decide that they don't wanna hate no more, they can look back on the fact that I'm different and I've done it, when they've got bored hating."

Dizzee claimed that he had moved on from his hate-filled early adolescence and found an outlet for his anger – his music. "Do I still feel [angry] now? Every now and then. However I feel at the time will come out in my music. It doesn't necessarily have to be angry. Right now I'm feeling quite happy. I'm not angry about too much right now, man." He did, however, concede that it was difficult for young men to extricate themselves from the violent London scene, rife as it was with gun crime, hence the regularity of such imagery cropping up in his songs. "About two or three years ago, more and more people started getting shot, there were more guns about," he explained. "Was it easy to get hold of a gun? It depends on who you are and how serious you are about getting them. It ain't just Bow or east London. Everybody knows there's a gun thing in this city."

London's reputation for gun crime had indeed begun to spread. Even Canadian website CBC ran a lengthy feature entitled 'Grime Wave', in which it explored in some depth the grim reality of life in east London and concluded that grime – "a bastard blend of street English, Jamaican dancehall reggae and two kinds of rave music: drum'n'bass, an electronic party monster built from breakbeats, or loops fashioned from the percussive 'breakdown' sections of other songs; and garage, which feels like R&B running a fever" – was the perfect soundtrack. The music, CBC explained to unversed Canadian readers, was notable for its "fast clatter of syncopated claps, alien chirps and machine bursts". Grime vocalists, it wrote, "resemble turbo-charged rappers, racing to match backing tracks that thump about 130 times per minute – near your target heart rate for vigorous physical activity". Meanwhile, grime itself was "clean and steely but filthy and ragged, all at once, like battlefield surgery... It is young, rebel music, with more songs about survival than love."

The article asserted that grime artists, like their audience, were predominantly young, black and male, and were raised in east London's low-income council estates. Their performances sometimes ended in what they called "ultraviolence", a tradition carried forward from the garage scene. Grime lyrics, meanwhile, were "laced with taunts directed at rival MCs" and grime concerts were organised as contests, or clashes, between competing crews. "On nights with bad voodoo in the air," CBC dramatically reported, "the clashes can turn to riots."

Dizzee Rascal, as the only grime star to achieve any "retail attention" on the other side of the Atlantic, spoke to CBC. He noted the need for grime after garage had "got to the point where it was almost 'bourgie' – suits, shoes". Grime came at just the right time for him. But then, the scene became overrun with guns and crime. "It turned really, really lawless," he said. "People definitely get shot, stabbed. London, especially right now, is a town where there's a lot of mad shit goin' on." He admitted that he had now "stepped out of that world".

He'd done so at just the right time, too. Like American hip hop 20 years earlier, UK grime was threatening to implode under the weight of its own messy internal strife, amid a welter of gang retribution and lethal violence. As *Blender* magazine wrote, "In the gentler British Isles, the kill rate may not be anywhere near as high [as in the States], but Dizzee's generation has witnessed a rapid increase in violence, gang culture, suicide, gun use and imprisonment. Their parents don't get it."

"It's fucked," said Dizzee of the east London area in which he grew up. He had good reason to say this, having seen his first dead body – a man killed by his wife – when he was 10 years old, and thereafter witnessed gun violence several times, including one occasion when a man was killed right in front of him at a rave. "There is a lot of shooting," he told *Blender*. "I've seen people getting shot, stabbed. All kinds of shit. It's not a game."

And yet he was determined not to revel in it all. He could see that it was a self-destructive route, and sensed that discussing it could make it become a self-fulfilling prophecy. On the inner sleeve to *Boy In Da Corner* he acknowledged the dangers all around him as well as "da fallen soldiers" whom he had lost along the way, but more importantly he struck a positive note when he said: "Keep grindin' – there's light at the end of the tunnel." For Dizzee, music was his beacon. As he affirmed at the time, a lot of hip hop was about rejoicing in the despair of one's surroundings, whereas what he wanted to do was bring some rays of light to bear on the scene. "A mistake with a lot of hip hop is the bombardment of that stuff," he said, insisting there was more to him than violence, gangs and guns. "I know other stuff as well."

CHAPTER 7

Mercury Rising

"I come from nothing – I come from the underground, pirate radio stations, I come from the ground, man. I want to thank God, my mum and my family and everyone in the underground."

Dizzee on winning the Mercury Prize

Most people, following an incident like the one experienced by Dizzee Rascal in Ayia Napa, would have crumbled, succumbed to depression, or perhaps even retaliated and thereby made a bad situation worse. Not Dizzee. He just got on with the business at hand: making the sort of music that was marking him out as the most original voice of his generation.

Speaking to Ben Thompson of *The Daily Telegraph* in 2009, Dizzee said that there had been "a lot of rehabilitation over the years", making it clear what he meant by this: "It's not like I went for counselling after getting stabbed, like most people would. I just kind of threw myself into my work and jumped into the public eye. I suppose from that perspective I'm quite lucky not to be strung out on heroin or something." There had been the occasional lapse, he admitted, presumably referring to the occasion of his arrest in late 2008 following a driving-related incident: "I have had the odd little moment, but on the whole I do a pretty good job of holding things together."

The year 2003 had been a real roller coaster of highs and lows for Dizzee. If July had been an absolute low point, September couldn't have been better – it was the month he beat 11 other highly acclaimed musicians to win the much-coveted Mercury Prize for best album of the year. He had already been lavished with awards for *Boy In Da Corner*: it was voted 2003's best album by ITV Teletext music page Planet Sound; it was chosen as one of the top 50 albums of the year by *Rolling Stone* alongside works by Kanye West, Mos Def, Eminem and Jadakiss; and he was given the *NME* Award for Innovation. But most prestigious of all was the Mercury, especially given the quality of the musicians he was up against: he beat everyone from Radiohead (nominated for *Hail To The Thief*) and Coldplay (*A Rush Of Blood To The Head*) to former Tricky sidekick Martina Topley-Bird (*Quixotic*) and left-field electronica favourites Lemon Jelly (*Lost Horizons*), not forgetting camp metal band The Darkness (*Permission To Land*).

Dizzee was the youngest person, at one month shy of his 18th birthday, to win the Mercury Prize, and only the second rapper, after Ms Dynamite, who had won the previous year. *The Independent*'s prediction a few months earlier, when *Boy In Da Corner* was first short-listed – "If it wins the Mercury and becomes the middle-class' annual 'street' purchase, a million dinner parties will grind to a halt" – was about to come true. Not that Dizzee himself saw it coming: in fact, he was apparently "so baffled by the whole situation" that he daubed question marks all over his jeans (he was still wearing those jeans several years later). He might not have been expecting to win, but he was happy to have been afforded the recognition – as much for himself as for the scene that spawned him. He told the BBC that the acknowledgement was important because, "I come from nothing – I come from the underground, pirate radio stations, I come from the ground, man." Receiving his award from the previous year's winner, Ms Dynamite, he said: "I want to thank God, my mum and

my family and everyone in the underground." The former Rinse
FM MC added: "Remember to support British talent – because it
is there."

The Mercury Prize, which is open to UK and Irish acts who
have released an album during the 12 months from June to June,
was, and remains, probably the most credible music award of
them all – far more so than the Brits, which many consider
to have an overly commercial and business-dictated agenda. It
has a reputation for backing non-established acts (more than
two-thirds of the winners of the prize had, by 2003, been for
début albums) across a myriad of genres. It is the award that best
reflects the content of the more serious music publications, and
a win means a seal of approval and virtual guarantee of further
acclaim from rock and dance music's cognoscenti. Some years,
the judges – who generally include journalists, DJs, academics
and composers – are accused of tokenist gestures in their choices
for the short list, ensuring as they do that categories such as jazz,
classical and folk are represented. And more than a few times
they have been lambasted for their choice of winner. But not the
year that Dizzee Rascal won. The unanimous opinion was that,
at London's Grosvenor House hotel on Tuesday September 8,
2003, the right artist won.

His former teacher, Tim Smith, certainly believed so – as soon as
he heard the news, he phoned Dizzee to offer his congratulations.
"He rang me this morning actually," Dizzee told a reporter. "He was
'nuff excited."

As for Dizzee, his reaction was one of pleasant puzzlement
– the council-estate pariah had been embraced by London's
mediarati. Unused to such glitzy surroundings, and perhaps
intoxicated by the Hennessy he had been drinking, he felt a
little disoriented. One account had it that he was expecting all
of the dozen nominees to win some prize or other, not just one
of them. And the last person he imagined would be picked as
outright winner would be himself, not with the likes of Coldplay
and Radiohead in the same contest. When 2002's winners Ms

Dynamite, came onstage to announce the winner, he fell silent. In his drunken state, he could barely believe what he'd heard. "Did she just say my name?" he wondered. But he wasn't hearing things. He had won.

He was baffled all right, and it was probably not just the thought of what he was now going to be able to do with the £20,000 prize, and where that money might take him. He later told *X-Ray* magazine that he had already begun to acquire, with his new extra cash, trainers, jackets, caps and Playstation games. But with wealth came a new sensible attitude towards money: whereas before he might have kept his loot in a shoe box under his bed, it was now safely locked away in a bank.

It was just the start. After four years toiling in the darkness, and on the margins, of London's nascent grime scene, the teenager was suddenly being talked about as Britain's most exciting new talent. Suddenly, he was the toast of the town, and all over the media like a rash. A reporter from *The Guardian*, calling him the next day to elicit his reaction, could hear him standing stunned in front of the television, bewildered to find himself a story on the lunchtime news as stray words from the TV presenter echoed down the phone line: "East London... garage MC... Mercury Prize." Dizzee simply paused, then laughed. "Shit, man," he said to the reporter. "They're discussing my future on the BBC. All these people talking, talking about me. I'm just like – carry on." He reflected for a moment, then added. "News, innit?"

At first, he hadn't wanted to come to the phone, somewhat taken aback as he was by the press scramble outside his mother's home. Dizzee's publicist had to reassure the journalist: "It's not that he doesn't want to do the interview," she explained, "but the press are outside his house. I think they want to talk to his mum. His brain's a bit scrambled at the moment."

When Dizzee finally did agree to talk, his bemusement was evident. It was perhaps understandable: it was only 12 hours since his win, and he was already having to come to terms with the fact that, as far as the media were concerned, as well as being a prodigiously gifted musician, songwriter and producer, he was also the first Mercury Prize winner to have lived a life every bit as gripping as his music.

The winners so far had either been routinely wayward, naughty indie boys (Suede, Primal Scream), polite mavericks (Badly Drawn Boy, PJ Harvey), unexciting musos of the dance (M People) or retro-rock variety (Gomez), or worthy but dull world music, drum'n'bass or rap-lite types (Talvin Singh, Roni Size, Ms Dynamite). The only remotely controversial, newsworthy winner thus far had been Jarvis Cocker, whose band, Pulp, won for their album *Different Class* in 1996. No sooner had he won than Cocker proceeded to hand over the award to Brian Eno and Tony Crean, the two men behind the Bosnian War Child album, *Help*, a project completed in 24 hours and one that had raised more than £2 million for charity. Michael Jackson's Brits nemesis told the stunned Mercury crowd: "In actual fact we've had our award already 'cos people bought a lot of copies of our album. We'd like to inaugurate a new music award right here tonight. The award is called The Pulp Music Award and there are two contestants in it: a record called *War Child* and a record called *Child Of War*. And the winner is... *War Child*."

Compared to the previous Mercury Prize recipients, then, Dizzee Rascal was hot stuff indeed, real hold-the-front-page business. Hence the clamour for his attention within minutes of winning, and hence his startled reaction to same.

"My head's all over the place," he admitted to Alexis Petridis, the journalist from *The Guardian*, when he eventually came to the phone. "People have been telling me it's like the most prestigious award. I'm starting to understand it more and more as I wake up. I'm getting more and more aware of what's going on now. I'm very, very, very, very happy about it, but it's a bit much, because I wasn't expecting it. I didn't expect it to get this much coverage, because it's grimy and the kind of audience it was aimed for isn't a massive audience. I always put people with my kind of background first. It's just amazing that it's reached so many people."

He might well have been amazed, but for Dizzee reaching a lot of people had always been the point. The intention had never been to simply make music to satisfy the grime underground. It wasn't world music that he was making – if anything, it was out of this world music – but he certainly wanted to make music for the world. In an interview with *The Independent* a month before the Mercury awards, he had told writer Nick Hasted of his desire for *Boy In Da Corner* to offer an insight into his corner of the world that the whole world could share and benefit from.

"It's to show people, maybe who even live where I do, what's going on around their corner," he said. "Adults just think they know, but they look at it from a newspaper point of view. I'm deep in, but I've got a brain, and I don't just want people from the estate or even the country I'm from to understand. I'm trying to give a perspective, from outside-in and inside-out. The best thing about the album is that there's loads of questions to be asked that haven't been asked before. I'm just saying this is what I know. This is the hand life dealt me, you know?"

When Hasted proposed to Dizzee that in coming to the attention of the world and being embraced by a wider audience his music might lose the very gritty quality that gave it its appeal in the first place, he was furious. He was especially angry at the complaint, made by The Streets' Mike Skinner (that other rap laureate and poet of the council estates and terraces), that since middle-class listeners had adopted him, garage fans wouldn't listen to him any more – the implication being that mainstream acceptance was synonymous with mediocrity and irrelevance.

"I've got nothing but respect for Mike Skinner, but he shouldn't worry about that, because progression is progression, and if garage people decide they don't like ya – that fan base ain't that big anyway," said Dizzee. "He's progressed to the middle classes, to make people understand him, but garage people still know who he is. It's the same with me. I ain't worried about, 'Oh, they're gonna think I'm not ghetto no more.' You can't tell me. The truth's there, and it's never going away. And I'm not here to be the most ghetto anyway; I don't give a shit about that. I'm making music now, and I can leave any time, man. The ones who go, 'I'm not leaving the ghetto', really it's because, deep down, they know they're never going to get a chance to. Why would anyone want to stay there?" Far from wanting to pander to a local elite, a narrow clique, Dizzee fully intended to appeal to America and beyond. "I was born in this little bit of rock, in the East End," he said. "But I'm in the world now."

CHAPTER 8

Graftin'

"I guess if anything you learn to appreciate life more when you nearly die."

Dizzee Rascal

izzee got busy after he won the Mercury Prize, which helped him take his place in the wider world. XL released a second single from *Boy In Da Corner* – 'Fix Up, Look Sharp' – giving him his first UK Top 20 entry. The CD release also included 'Stop Dat' and the video for first single 'I Luv U', which featured an extra portion of music not on the original version of the song. The video that accompanied his second single appeared to have been directed by the same team who designed the début album sleeve – namely, graphic artist Gareth Bayliss and associates – with its stark black and yellow colour scheme and similar typography. But it was actually Ruben Fleischer, director of music videos, TV commercials and short films. Frenetic and fast cut to match the music, it presented Dizzee as the hyperactive city kid in a variety of urban outfits, hoodies, track suits and baseball caps, making shapes and moving in front of the camera with an ease that suggested he was born to do this.

It was filmed, explained Dizzee, in Los Angeles, where he had the time of his life, hardly surprising considering it was his first ever foreign sortie. "I went to LA and it was rah!" he gushed. "It was another world. I came back and my head felt clear. The vibe was amazing."

'Fix Up, Look Sharp' peaked at number 17 in August 2003, spending three weeks inside the Top 40 and five inside the Top 75. It had a considerable afterlife in terms of its appearances in popular culture, its numerous remixes and use in sampled form. It was also featured in the hit documentary *Rize* (about dance subcultures in Los Angeles) and on an episode of controversial British teen drama *Skins*, and appeared briefly in the US hit show about Superboy, *Smallville*, in the episode entitled 'Velocity'. Just as the song heavily sampled the main beat and vocals from 'The Big Beat' by American rocker Billy Squier, so 'Fix Up, Look Sharp' was in turn sampled by playful UK hip hop/electronica duo Dan Le Sac Vs Scroobius Pip for their song 'Fixed', and was remixed by New York experimentalists Ratatat for their *Ratatat Remixes Vol. 1* mix-tape. And it appeared in the video game 'DJ Hero' in various remixed forms.

In November 2003, a third track was lifted from *Boy In Da Corner* for UK single release: 'Jus' A Rascal', which became his third Top 40 hit, peaking at number 30 and spending three weeks inside the Top 75. As with the previous single, the three-track CD included a 'clean' version for radio, the original album version, plus a video, this time the one for 'Fix Up, Look Sharp'. The video for 'Jus' A Rascal' itself was a slight departure – instead of a studio, it showed Dizzee being filmed on a boat going across the Thames with several dozen revellers, both male (including another rising grime star, Tinchy Stryder, who made a cameo appearance) and female – even though this was London, it resembled a US rap party video. It was also quintessentially "teen" and exuded late-night menace – perfect soundtrack music, then, for *Skins*, on which it earned Dizzee another appearance for one of his singles. It was subsequently also used on the soundtrack to *Kidulthood*, the highly acclaimed 2006 British film drama about teenagers in west London.

Dizzee scored a double in November 2003 when he collaborated with premier London dance duo and XL labelmates Basement Jaxx on a track called 'Lucky Star' (which also featured Indian actress and model Mona Singh), for their third album, *Kish Kash*. 'Lucky Star' was released as a 12-inch single and gave Dizzee a fourth Top 30 hit, peaking at number 23, the same position reached by *Boy In Da Corner*. A fourth track from the album, 'Jezebel', was never officially released as a single, but it did prove popular on the underground circuit.

Also helping Dizzee gain exposure in the wider world were his live performances. He had hit the ground running with regard to gigs, having been invited to support the world's biggest rapper, Jay-Z, at Wembley Stadium around the release of 'I Luv U'. His Mercury Prize win immediately gained him access to audiences far beyond his grime-y east London roots. Almost inevitably, the prediction made by *The Independent* that he was about to become the darling of the middle-class set came true when, in March 2004, he was booked to perform at London's Royal Festival Hall.

One reviewer, there that night, noted that, "Worlds collided when the ghetto street sounds of Dizzee Rascal's crew played a venue normally accustomed to more reserved performances from classical musicians." The stage was set up to create a "street atmosphere", with a menacing red and black glow, the DJ's decks uplit by cold blue light coming from the floor, and further green circles of light creating a stark but striking backdrop.

Dizzee opened his set, just as he did his album, with 'Sittin' Here', for which he stood up and instructed the culturally diverse audience in the prim surrounds of the RFH to do the same, proclaiming, "This ain't no sit down thing". Requesting that they "listen faster", he proceeded to treat the assembled – "a uniquely polarised fan base: half pirate radio listeners from Hackney and half subscribers to the *Wire*", according to another journalist, this one from *The Guardian* – to some fast-rapping pyrotechnics, as a result whipping them up into a frenzy. Already something of a showman, Dizzee indulged in some crowd participation, although, perhaps embarrassed to be so active in the relatively staid environs of the RFH (relative to an east London club, say), not many joined in. "You people are gonna respect me if it kills me," he warned (although it was actually a lyric from a new track entitled 'Respect Me', from his forthcoming second album, *Showtime*). A few people at the front rushed to shake his hand but the crowd's reaction was muted if appreciative, moving Dizzee to shout: "I can't hear you!" The gig ended, however, on a high, with an encore of 'Fix Up, Look Sharp', even Dizzee neophytes recognising his biggest hit single. Nevertheless, the first reviewer couldn't help feeling that "Dizzee belongs to the street – his razor-sharp tongue sounded out of place in an arena used to hearing orchestras play." He concluded: "That he was invited to play at the Royal Festival Hall at all is testament to his award-winning talent... But he should be seen in a venue with a character matching his own." Or as the man from *The Guardian,* Dorian Lynskey, wryly put it: "By ignoring his surroundings rather than exploiting them, Dizzee gives the impression of some calamitous booking mix-up. You wonder if, at this very moment, members of the London Sinfonietta are nervously tuning up in a warehouse in Bow."

A month earlier, on a freezing cold night in February, Dizzee had made his US concert début in a far more suitable venue – Volume, a new club in the hip Williamsburg area of Brooklyn, New York. It was good timing: *Boy In Da Corner* had just been released in the States and was considered by many hip hop aficionados in America to be a breath of fresh UK air blasting through the stultified US rap scene. "Given the relative monotony of American commercial hip hop radio, one would have to wonder if a kid from the streets of London with a rubbery British accent would have even half a chance of competing against the likes of the Family Roc or Lil Jon's ever-expanding clique," wrote journalist Michael Crumsho of *Dusted* magazine. "However, based upon his début American performance at Volume, one would be inclined to think that the spins are his for the taking."

The club – nestled near the East River among several other industrial-type warehouses – was considered to have a slightly sterile atmosphere, and there were no stages, leaving performers in the smaller of the two rooms where the British rapper was about to appear to roam about the floor. Meanwhile, the larger room's spotlight fell on the back of an 18-wheeler flatbed truck. When they saw Dizzee Rascal climb onto the truck, the audience, who had come in their droves to "evaluate the hype" about this Britrap wunderkind and his "grimy soundscapes", erupted. He seemed apprehensive at first, somewhat startled, perhaps, by the excitable reaction to his music, written two years earlier at home in Bow, from a crowd several thousand miles away in Brooklyn. But from the incendiary rendition of 'I Luv U' onwards, there was no let-up, no pause in the pressure, as Dizzee overcame his US first-night nerves to prove himself a true master of ceremonies. He whipped the crowd up, stalked the stage, traded quips and made sure hands remained in the air. According to Crumsho, Dizzee stuck mostly to material from *Boy In Da Corner* and "breathed new stage life" into the likes of 'Stop Dat', dazzling allcomers with his rhythmic dexterity and lyrical virtuosity.

He even sprinkled freestyle a cappellas throughout the "unfortunately brief" set, thereby, wrote Crumsho, "rebuffing any that dared doubt his flow or ample skills as an MC". He had the ideal opportunity to prove his chops in this area when, during a climactic version of 'Brand New Day', the record began skipping. "Unfazed and with a smile on his face, Rascal instructed his DJ (Slim) to cut the music and then proceeded to finish the song sans instrumental," remarked Crumsho, comparing Dizzee's powers of spontaneous invention to those of KRS-One, that pioneer of rap "edutainment".

All in all, it was a successful first foray to the States, one that made it clear Dizzee's music, born in such a different place, could transcend geography and cultural specificity. Indeed, it was his very difference that appealed, as Crumsho wrote: "Aside from mic skills, Dizzee also brought a refreshingly subdued confidence with him on stage, saving all masturbatory boasts and self-references... In this era of shiny MCs and constant rhymes about jewellery and clothes, such an introspective voice [was] welcome."

The super-positive response to Dizzee Rascal Stateside was echoed by the *NME* when its reporter caught him live at the Irving Plaza in New York a few months later, in summer 2004. It was a joint display by Britrap's two hotshots, headlined as it was by Mike Skinner aka The Streets. But it was, according to writer Elizabeth Goodman, Dizzee who stole the show. The venue reeked of "cheap perfume worn by chicks ordering Malibu and Diet Coke" paid for by their "backwards-cap-sporting boyfriends" as Dizzee strode out before the sold-out, 2,000-capacity crowd in his Yankees cap, gleaming white sneakers and blue jeans decorated with a thick white stripe on the rear resembling a giant, heart-shaped bull's eye. "The diamond stud in his ear glints in the spotlight as his lips part and a rapid stream of incomprehensible words come tumbling out," she enthused, the crowd's rapturous response making it seem as though Jay-Z himself was in the house. One particularly reverent worshipper at the altar of the Rascal, among the assembled "freaks and geeks", began bowing down in a we-are-not-worthy manner. Dizzee's every last Bow-derived bon mot and serrated rhyme was lapped up by the NYC massive, who "screamed themselves hoarse". After this, Mike Skinner didn't stand a chance. "Though both artists are touring behind brilliant records," decided Goodman, "tonight it's Dizzee Rascal who brings that brilliance alive onstage."

Most onlookers were amazed at Dizzee's excellence as a performer. Some commentators were amazed for different reasons – amazed at the lack of violence at his concerts, especially given the Ayia Napa affair and his general reputation as the bad boy of British rap. "People can always speculate, so you might as well let them," he told a reporter. "One thing I can say is that I've never been short of drama in my life. I'm not even gonna lie, a lot of things have happened. But it hasn't stopped me from doing what I'm doing – so that's all good, innit!" The reporter pressed him on the point, suggesting that speculation was hardly surprising considering the violent image garage music had been afforded in the media. Dizzee disagreed, explaining that it was the audience that was angry: the music catered to the need for an outlet for their rage: "It's not the music that's violent," he said. He took the opportunity to compare garage and grime to earlier rebel musics with an insurrectionary agenda. "People talk about it that way because they don't fully understand it. Garage is something that was cultivated and made by people from the streets, the have–nots. Like drum'n'bass was. Like punk. When something's that close to the streets, in the inner city, people go to clubs and sometimes they don't get along and sometimes people end up getting hurt. That's the negative side. With time, as it grows, it will get better. The positive side, though, is that people who might not have had a chance in life have gone out and made something for themselves. And people don't get shot and stabbed at Dizzee Rascal concerts. I ain't seen one yet!"

If Dizzee was undeniably busy in the wake of the success of *Boy In Da Corner*, there was some doubt as to how happy that success had made him. Alexis Petridis of *The Guardian* found him "curiously uncomfortable" with it all, surmising that this might have been because, foreign trips aside, his success had yet to bring about a radical change of circumstance or lifestyle. "My real friends are still the same," he said. "We go out, we do whatever. It's as confusing for them as it is for you. People see you on the TV and that, and they forget that you're from the streets. All the public things that you get, success and other things, there's another side that people might not know too much about. They might think you're just saying these things in your lyrics. Shit does happen; you really experience these things on the streets, and success – that can be a problem. A gift and a curse, you know what I mean?"

In an interview with *X-Ray* magazine, he was asked whether he was happy as he contemplated his achievements so far. "Yeah, man," he said, vaguely. "I'm alive for a start, innit? Some people, they go to sleep, and don't ever wake up." What, asked journalist Lulu Le Vay, had he learned from his experiences so far? "Ah, I dunno," he replied. "To live life and not spend your life moaning. I do moan, don't get me wrong! But I moan while I'm getting on with things! I've got friends who moan all the time and they sit in the same spot for years and years and years – that's not real living. Everyone is here for something. You got to follow what you do to the neck, to the end of it!" The reason for his philosophical approach to life was clear: "I guess if anything you learn to appreciate life more," he said, "when you nearly die."

It was a good attitude, and all that remained was to ask whether this gifted, troubled, complex boy from the ghetto had the courage to continue to expose the "dark and scary shit", as Le Vay put it, that there appeared to be inside his head; and whether he had what it took, after all the sudden fame and acclaim, awards and first-class foreign travel, to keep it up. Basically, was he already suffering from the what-to-do-next second album syndrome? After *Boy In Da Corner*, what on earth was he going to do for an encore?

"I can't lie, it might be there," he admitted of his fear, "but it's what you decide to focus on. It's either 'got-to-do-this-got-to-do-this!'" he said, miming panic, "or, 'I'm going to do this calmly and give it to them, like I did with the first one'."

CHAPTER 9

Respect Me

"Music is music, no matter where you come from. Everyone should be able to make any kind of music."

Dizzee Rascal

The first new music issued in the wake of *Boy In Da Corner* came in August 2004, just over 12 months after the début album – not long in this day and age, when gaps between releases can often be a matter of years. It was the single 'Stand Up Tall' and it was the first release from Dizzee Rascal's second album, due in September 2004, to be titled *Showtime*.

With writing credited to 'D Mills' and co-produced by Youngsta, a London dubstep DJ, and Nick Cage, 'Stand Up Tall' was based on an unknown rave or electro sample and featured an infectious beat and melody as well as a message of self-empowerment, advising listeners to pull themselves up by their bootstraps, just as he had done. It referenced the music journalists across the globe who applauded him, heard Dizzee comparing himself favourably to US rapper Nelly and proceeded to instruct wannabe Dizzees to get their finger out if they wanted to achieve even a modicum of his success.

The video found Dizzee stepping out of a silver-grey London cab but clearly not in London (it was Atlanta, Georgia), accompanied by four young girls dressed variously in sexily customised versions of policewoman and beefeater outfits, reclaiming the Union Jack and dancing wildly in various locations, including a bar, a diner, a barber's shop and a pole-dancing club. It was again directed by Ruben Fleischer, who offered a treatment for the video to the record company. In it, he proposed Atlanta as the location because he had just shot a KFC commercial down there and, as he said, "It is the place to be, it is much cheaper than LA to shoot there, there is no shortage of beautiful black women to be found... And, last but not least, it is the strip-club capital of the United States." He also wanted to capture the feel of "Dirty South" rap videos and the aim was for it to be "100 per cent authentic and tough".

The original plan was to use lots of "quintessentially British 'bling' items", particularly classic luxurious and/or collectible vintage British cars such as E-Type Jaguars, Bentleys and Land Rovers, but in the end budget constraints limited Fleischer to just the silver-grey London cab. As for the women, the director aimed to use "the same hot video bitches that we see in the Ludacris and Nelly videos, only maybe one will be dressed as a sexy 'bobby', another is dressed like Lady Di or the Queen... Everyone will be super blinged-out and look hot and hype." Those Princess Diana and QEII lookalikes didn't actually transpire in the finished video; nevertheless, the important thing, he said, was to use some elements from US rap promos while simultaneously establishing Dizzee's apartness from his American peers. "I just want to make sure that there is a real link to the UK so that we can distinguish Dizzee from the typical American hip hop dudes."

His detailed proposal worked: 'Stand Up Tall' became Dizzee's fourth consecutive Top 40 hit, and highest-charting entry to date, entering at number 10 and spending six weeks inside the UK Top 75. It was also the first of his singles to be released on two CDs. The first featured 'Stand Up Tall' and another track called 'Give U More' (featuring rapper D Double E of Newham Generals), which was far more in the spirit of angular, futurist invention displayed on *Boy In Da*

Corner than the lead track, which rather looked forward to the more straightforward dance-pop sound of his late-Noughties hits with 'Bonkers', 'Dance Wiv Me' and 'Holiday'. The second CD featured five versions of the single, including a radio edit, an instrumental, a 'Youngsta Remix Instrumental' and an a cappella version. The track later appeared on the EA Sports video game *FIFA Street* and in the 2005 Steve Carell movie, *The 40-Year-Old Virgin*. Six years later, on *Jools Holland's 2010 Hootenanny* British television show, Dizzee would perform a radically different version of 'Stand Up Tall' over the backing track music of Nirvana's 'Smells Like Teen Spirit', a favourite song from his youth. In fact, it was around the time of the release of 'Stand Up Tall' that he expressed his enthusiasm for the grunge overlords, especially their tragic frontman, Kurt Cobain, with whom he felt a deep connection.

"I sense such a free spirit from someone like Kurt Cobain," he said. "I didn't really know what he was talking about, but he was a bit messed up, y'know! People like him look rough and they smash things up. 'Smells Like Teen Spirit' was a tune, man! But then I looked at my own stuff and I can see some similarities. They [Nirvana] were just supposed to be grunge, innit? But they weren't. Music is music, no matter where you come from. Everyone should be able to make any kind of music."

In September 2004, on his second album, Dizzee demonstrated his ongoing commitment to pursuing his eclectic vision. Self-produced like its predecessor, the album featured an array of stunning sounds and samples, culled from a variety of sources, although it was hard to dispel the disappointment that it failed to deliver any shock of the new this time. But then, it was hardly Dizzee's fault his début album was such a revelation. Album opener 'Showtime' was the shortest track at two minutes and 12 seconds. Over a slow rhythm, Dizzee announced himself, playing on his name and referencing the album title. He proceeded to tell his story, although for the track he assumed, for some unknown reason, the name "Ray". His tale began over half a decade earlier, ran the lyric, on a dilapidated east London estate and followed him through his stints on pirate radio by night and struggles to keep up with school work by day. It emphasised how he was less concerned with the trappings of success than he was with the music itself and reminded listeners of his adolescence, one that had been rife with drama. After the single, 'Stand Up Tall', came 'Everywhere', which resembled one of Timbaland's productions for Missy Elliot with its tablas and jerky tempo. The lyric was a typically Dizzee-ish tumble of words about the harshness of existence, full of near-comical bravado and common-sense assertions. 'Graftin'' which would be his sixth single (another track from *Showtime*, 'Dream', was his fifth), was a slow, grinding affair; suitably, the lyrics spoke about London in poetic terms and presented the image of the city as a surreal nightmarescape prowled by Dizzee on the make, trying to succeed even though, like the bluesmen before him, he had a hellhound on his trail. 'Learn' harked back to the Far Eastern flavours of *Boy In Da Corner*, only this time it was the beats, not the melody and texture of the music, that were infused with essence of the Orient. Lyrically, it was another autobiographical number, with references to his support slot at Wembley with Jay-Z, and there were intimations of an alternate future where he hadn't had a successful, award-winning début album. There was also an overall sense of spite towards his haters, which started to seem a little like sour grapes, or at least failed to convince, especially when you considered the year he'd just enjoyed. 'Hype Talk' was, save for the pretty glockenspiel motif and what sounded like a beatbox rhythm, nearly a cappella. Again, it dealt with his recent story, including the Ayia Napa incident asking whether Wiley did indeed leave him behind there and if he did hit Mega in the face. It also addressed the moans he had to face on the street, or in the media, from gossip-mongers and detractors who resented his success. 'Face' (featuring Caramel) included references to Megaman, fellow grime artists Lethal Bizzle and the Nasty Crew, and presented a picture of Dizzee the put-upon star, besieged by phone calls and requests for favours, hangers-on trying to capitalise on his fame, swamped by jealous types and haters, as well as women who only want him for his money. Despite the line about feeling the vibe and appreciating his love, and acknowledgment of the difficulty his detractors were having coming to terms with his success, this was another track that left a bitter taste in the mouth, the cameo from Caramel as the catty chav undesirable adding to the atmosphere of vengeful misanthropy.

Then there was 'Respect Me', the longest track at four minutes and 45 seconds, which was either a sustained burst of electronic menace or an overlong tirade aimed at those who were blaming him for, among other things, gun crime, as well as a warning to women who wrongly assumed he was now an easy target for their attentions. His rap was full of nonchalant asides, but it was evident that people's opinions were actually cutting him to the quick. 'Get By', featuring R&B warbler Vanya on the mellifluous chorus, was another track that recalled the pretty Oriental melodies from the début album. It was also another of his reminiscences about his rough childhood of which, paradoxically, he had fond memories. This time he handed over the mournful, emotional chorus to Vanya and for once on *Showtime* Dizzee expressed, rather than enmity, feelings of empathy for the people he'd left behind on the estates, from criminals to young baby mothers, although the pay-off line smacked a little of I'm-all-right-Jack, recommending that people in downtrodden estates should just up sticks and leave, to which one could easily have responded, "That's easy for you to say, mate". 'Knock Knock' found Dizzee anointing himself Public Enemy Number One, the rapper whom kids' parents love to hate, and dreaming of revenge for all those bouncers at the posh garage clubs who refused him entry for wearing the wrong shoes when he was an up-and-coming pirate radio star. It also found him for the umpteenth time on *Showtime* parading his Ayia Napa war wounds with a pride verging on relish, with references to his stab wounds and the way they helped, as he saw it, raise his profile. Spartan but hardly striking, when Dizzee proclaimed during the song that he was here to annoy and remove all joy, it was tempting to agree with him.

The final third of the album saw a considerable improvement. 'Dream' was a departure into poppy territory, featuring as it did a prominent sample of the kiddie chorus from 'Happy Talk'. This had been a 1982 number one hit for Captain Sensible, formerly the guitarist with punk rockers The Damned, which was itself a cover version of the song from the 1949 Rodgers and Hammerstein musical *South Pacific*. As such it recalled his US rap hero Jay-Z's breakthrough single 'Hard Knock Life', which used a sample from children's musical *Annie*. Whether or not it was a concerted bid to further Dizzee's mainstream ambitions, it certainly did the trick when it was issued as a single in November 2004: it became his second consecutive Top 20 entry and longest-running one, staying in the Top 75 for eight weeks. To match the saccharine sample, Dizzee came over all sympathetic on this track, preaching self-belief of the "you can make it if you try" variety that was worthy of Louis Walsh on *The X Factor*, advising young listeners to be attentive at school, promising to look out for those on the breadline and generally coming over as though 'Dream' was a sort of latter-day, grime-age 'Greatest Love Of All'. 'Girls' (featuring rapper Marga Man) was virtually a comedy interlude, detailing Dizzee's success with the ladies since finding fame, only doing so with humorous exaggeration that somehow managed to avoid accusations of misogyny, presumably by dint of its almost *Carry On*-ishly comical air. It also provided a musical respite from the slow, grinding numbers, being a fast, stuttering rave track that harked back to acid house, only with the rhythmic tricksiness of modern R&B. 'Imagine' was arguably the album's highlight. It found Dizzee, in abrupt contrast to the previous track, in a wistful mood, wondering about the contradictions of a lifetime's pursuit of the authentic. Here, after all, was a musician for whom "keeping it real" was the ultimate stamp of approval, but whose very documentation of the gritty and everyday provided a passport out of the so-called ghetto. The lyric heard him wonder aloud whether leaving behind his manor for bigger, fresher pastures would amount to a sell-out. It was a reasonable question to ask even if it failed to provide an answer, and the music was as wrenchingly pretty as Japan (the early Eighties new romantic band, not the country).

The penultimate track, 'Flyin'', set the record straight: Dizzee was, he insisted, the same as he ever was, the straight-talking boy from the hood, and no amount of fame and acclaim would ever alter that. Album closer 'Fickle' was, musically, as close as anything on *Showtime* to melodramatic US-style thug rap; lyrically, it was a veritable onslaught of language, almost a thousand words' worth, but the most telling part was the coda, which intimated that Dizzee's new-found success had left him feeling strangely alienated and bereft, perhaps wondering whether the loss of credibility in some quarters was hardly worth all the benefits, the money and attention from the ladies.

Depending on your vantage point, *Showtime* was either a consolidation of Dizzee Rascal's achievements on *Boy In Da Corner* or a reiteration, while the lyrics, typically of not just second-album releases by rappers but rockers as well, found the artist reflecting on the merits of his new-found status as a wealthy, successful musician with foreign travel now *de rigueur* and legions of yes-men at his beck and call. It was an album made in the wake of success that was as much about that transition as anything else, and as such one either found it winning or wearing. Even die-hards would have been hard pressed to deny that, after 15 tracks and 51 minutes of it, the relentless self-referencing was a bit much.

The *NME*, to name one organ of the press, found it lyrically "astonishing", which was a bit of a stretch even if you were feeling generous. Retro rock monthly *MOJO* focused more on the music and decided that, "What Dizzee Rascal has done with this record is find his own — profoundly satisfying — balance between grime's digital vortex of ringtones and car alarms and an older more contemplative electronic tradition." *The Guardian* was equally positive in its assessment, journalist Dorian Lynskey finding greatness in the record's ambivalence and declaring it "both a triumphant throwdown and a sardonic dig at his new-found status". Lynskey located precedents for self-referential second-album comeback single 'Stand Up Tall' in Eminem's 'The Real Slim Shady' and Tricky's 'Tricky Kid', declaring Dizzee's effort "colossal... witty, knowing, and swaggering like Godzilla". Elsewhere on the album he praised Dizzee's "playful defiance" in the face of his detractors, as well as his self-awareness, detecting light-heartedness where others might have seen self-indulgent whingeing. He also noted a "recurring obsession with insular scene politics", but suggested these were more than made up for by the "surprising and compelling sonic twists", concluding that there was now no stopping "the most dextrous and quotable MC Britain has ever produced".

In America, where they arguably took Dizzee Rascal even more seriously than they did in the UK, *Spin* magazine was moved to declare *Showtime* "a classic sophomore album in the hip hop sense: puffy with bluster, brimming with indignation". Website Lost At Sea called it "one of the finest pieces of pop music to drop this decade". Pop Matters noted the difficulty of following up "one of the most highly praised, incendiary, ground-breaking and influential albums of the decade", one that crammed a lifetime's amount of work and ambition into a single record, and acknowledged that, like most second albums, *Showtime* concerned two subjects: "being famous, and how much it sucks (or rules) to be famous". And yet, enhanced by a denser sound, the "touches of dancehall, African percussion, glitch pop, Eighties electro, and Far Eastern influences" and the increased use of melodic flourishes, these songs about the price of fame, offset by some sly humour, worked. It even found 'Girls' "deliciously lecherous" and concluded that, "underneath all the bravado is a contemplative side to Dizzee Rascal that remains his greatest asset."

There were some negative reviews. All Music decried the "slightly noxious lechery of 'Girls'" and found that "a few too many rhymes about his past year in the spotlight are simple-minded and needlessly defensive". It did, however, go on to say that "you can still get lost in the pure sound of his voice – an attraction as serious as his production prowess" and that, "As a beatmaker, Dizzee now ranks near the top, entire planet considered, whether he's dishing out a crowd-hyping batter-bounce or crafting something more intricate, where synthetic approximations of exotic instrumentation – Oriental melodies, African percussion – are pitted against ballast-blasting beats." Pitchfork cited some "patronising and grating" examples of rock star griping, from Pink Floyd's 'Money' to Pink's 'Don't Let Me Get Me', but suggested that *Showtime* was closer to Nirvana's *In Utero*, which Dizzee once proclaimed his favourite album of all time, in the way it wrestled with doubts about a fame he had once so arduously courted. In summing up, the influential website decided that *Showtime* "naturally lacks the shock of the new, the jolt of *Boy In Da Corner*" but that "instead, it's a consolidation of his strengths, lyrically and sonically, and a more satisfying listen than its predecessor; much more muscular and confident". *Blender* was less munificent, concluding that *Showtime* was "a slower, grimmer album [than *Boy In Da Corner*]... Fame and misfortune have driven Dizzee further into his favourite place: his skull."

In terms of chart positions, *Showtime* eclipsed the achievement of its predecessor, entering at number eight. It was soon certified gold by the British Phonographic Industry (BPI), selling over 100,000 copies in the UK, although it did less well in the States than *Boy In Da Corner*, shifting just over 16,000 units there compared to the 58,000 copies sold of the début.

Second albums, though, can enjoy short-term success but do little for the artist in the long term. It remained to be seen whether *Boy In Da Corner* would ultimately be regarded as the peak of Dizzee Rascal's brief career, or whether he had already burrowed too deep into his brain to ever find a way out.

CHAPTER 10

Everywhere

"People say I'm selling out but it doesn't get to me any more. There's no point trying to prove how hard or underground I am. I'm going with what feels natural at this point."

Dizzee Rascal

As 2004 proceeded, it was evident that Dizzee Rascal was simply too busy to succumb to solipsism, and if accusations of water-treading on his second album, *Showtime*, had affected him, he wasn't showing it. In October 2004 it was reported in *NME* that he had been working with Beck and that he had remixed a new track by the US pop polymath for future single release. Dizzee, then about to embark on his first major tour of the UK, told the music weekly's website: "I've just finished a remix for Beck – it's a song called 'Hell, Yeah' and I'm very excited about that. It happened easily – he asked and naturally I said 'yes'. He's a credible artist, a real artist, so I'm happy."

In November, he released 'Dream', his second single from *Showtime* and fifth overall. It came with several other tracks on the CD (a live version of 'Imagine' recorded earlier that year in Austin, Texas, plus two brand new tunes: 'Is This Real?', a song about how he got high to keep calm, and a particularly strong number called 'Trapped' that would have benefitted *Showtime* had it been included on that album). The video reflected the almost infantile positivism of the lyric, and expanded upon the kiddie chorus sampled from Captain Sensible's 'Happy Talk'. It was an artful re-creation of a *Watch With Mother*-style Fifties or Sixties kids' TV show, hosted by a prim, old-fashioned middle-aged lady sitting at a piano.

"Hello, boys and girls, I wonder what Dizzee Rascal is up to today? He's such a rascal," she announces at the beginning in her poshest BBC received-pronunciation voice. She starts playing the piano and the song begins as Dizzee appears out of a children's music box. Various break-dancing hoodie marionettes proceed to re-enact our hero's childhood reminiscences about gun crime and pirate radio shenanigans, as though it were a ghetto version of *Andy Pandy*. Thereafter in the video, two puppet men steal a TV, and the puppet police arrive in a police car to apprehend the puppet thieves; another puppet spray-paints a shop wall; a pint-sized Dizzee walks into a disco and raps in a recording studio; and two puppets pass by pushing their babies in prams, all on top of the woman's piano.

These were all depictions of images or events from Dizzee's life, although what the dancing ostrich had to do with his experiences in grim east London isn't clear. Dougal Wilson's puppet-laden video for 'Dream' achieved some renown on the web, perhaps for its cuteness, while for Dizzee it was fun, even if he did feel a little anxious having to act alongside puppet animals. "I dreaded it," he said of filming the promo. "It was weird, because there was nothing to act with; there were just the puppets. It was good, though, it was a learning experience." People seemed to like it: 'Dream' became his fifth Top 40 hit and second consecutive Top 20 entry, peaking at number 14, his second-highest position. It also became his longest-running single up to that point, spending eight weeks inside the Top 75.

His next release, 'Graftin'', by contrast, released in March 2005, became his lowest-charting single and his first to miss the Top 40, peaking at number 44, despite being a double A-side with another strong brand new track, 'Off 2 Work', which was so spartan that the rapid-fire words effectively provided the staccato rhythm. For this release – almost a concept double A-side about the importance of hustle and hard graft – both songs came with their own videos. The one that accompanied 'Off 2 Work' was as light and frothily entertaining as a Madness romp, featuring Dizzee in a variety of banal workplace scenarios (businessman, fitness instructor, pounding the beat as a traffic warden, cutting meat in a kebab shop) before assuming the suited-and-booted role of Prime Minister on the day that he announces his engagement to a woman called Sherie Blair, who happens to bear a striking resemblance to former PM Tony Blair's other half. The 'Graftin'' promo was far grimier and grittier, some of it filmed indoors – Dizzee surrounded by friends and subsumed by smoke in the tiny, dark front room of an inner-city flat – and some of it filmed at night outside, beneath a grim tower block of the sort he would have been familiar with from his youth (it was directed by Goetz Werner in Bow, where Dizzee grew up).

The 'Dream' single did well enough even if 'Graftin'' was a commercial disappointment, but sandwiched between both releases was something far more impressive. Because during Christmas 2004, Dizzee Rascal found himself for the very first time in his career – but by no means the last – at number one in the UK charts. Towards the end of the year, he was invited to be involved in Band Aid 20, an updated version – v 2.0, in computer parlance – of 'Do They Know It's Christmas?', the best-selling charity recording from 1984, which had raised millions for Ethiopian famine victims and led to the landmark Live Aid concert extravaganza of summer 1985. The re-recorded track, written as was the original by Band Aid (and Live Aid) prime movers Bob Geldof and Midge Ure, was designed to benefit Sudan's troubled Darfur region, with all money raised going to the famine relief fund. It was to be performed by a new incarnation of the Band Aid group, with U2's Bono, Paul McCartney and George Michael the only artists remaining from the original recording.

The project's organiser was the former Ultravox frontman Midge Ure, and the producers were Nigel Godrich (producer of

Radiohead's best albums) and Bob Geldof, while Damon Albarn of Blur and Gorillaz was reputedly on hand to serve tea and biscuits to all the participants. The musicians comprised some of the biggest names in mid-Noughties pop, rock, R&B and dance – notably, playing the instruments in the band, Danny Goffey of Supergrass on drums, Radiohead's Thom Yorke and Jonny Greenwood on, respectively, piano and guitar, Sir Paul on bass, and Justin Hawkins of The Darkness on guitar; while on vocals, singing those famous lines about solving poverty and world famine, there were, among numerous others, Bono, Natasha Bedingfield, Chris Martin of Coldplay, Ms Dynamite, members of Keane, Snow Patrol and Sugababes, and pop idols Busted and Will Young, as well as Dido (performing from a studio in Melbourne) and Robbie Williams (who sang his part from a studio in Los Angeles).

Dizzee Rascal made history by being the first artist since its original release to add new lyrics to the song, which – again, uniquely – he rapped instead of singing. His two lines, improvised on the spot according to producer Godrich, were pithily in keeping with the charity theme. The track was recorded on November 14, and released later that same month. It was first played simultaneously on *The Chris Moyles Show* on Radio 1 and the breakfast shows on Virgin and Capital radio stations, at 8am on November 16, while the video was first broadcast in the UK on a variety of channels, including the five UK terrestrial ones, two days later at exactly 5.55pm, with an introduction by none other than Madonna. In this, the early days of download purchasing, it could be bought from Apple's iTunes music store, the computer company donating an amount to the Band Aid Trust.

The single's sleeve was designed by controversial British artist Damien Hirst, whose original startling cover for the Band Aid 20 single featured the grim reaper and a starving African child. It was, however, deemed too shocking and later dropped amid fears that it might scare the very people it was aimed at – children. With a new, more benign painted sleeve of a doe-eyed deer in a Christmassy scene, it sold 72,000 copies in the first 24 hours of its

"LA was another world." Dizzee in California, March 2003. (JAMIE BEEDEN/CORBIS OUTLINE)

Executive producer Midge Ure, Justin Hawkins of The Darkness and Dizzee recording the remake of charity single 'Do They Know It's Christmas?' at Air Studios, Hampstead on November 14, 2004. (DAVE HOGAN/GETTY IMAGES)

Dizzee recording Band Aid 20.

(TOM OLDHAM/REX FEATURES)

Live at Manchester Academy on February 19, 2008. (SHIRLAINE FORREST/WIREIMAGE)

DJ Semtex in full FX mode. (NAKI/REDFERNS)

At the MTV Australia Awards 2008. (KRISTIAN DOWLING/GETTY IMAGES)

Dizzee in 2007. (TOM OLDHAM/REX FEATURES)

Onstage in Sydney on January 24, 2010. (GRAHAM DENHOLM/WIREIMAGE)

Arriving at the *NME* Awards in 2009. (MARC LARKIN/LFI)

Dizzee in July 2003, his *annus mirabilis* – except for Ayia Napa. (LFI)

release on November 29, and entered the charts at number one on December 5. The CD version sold over 200,000 copies in the first week, and became the fastest-selling (and biggest-selling) single of the year, remaining at pole position for Christmas and the week after, holding on to the top spot for four weeks in total – just one week fewer than the original had done 20 years earlier.

There was even a special documentary to go with the single entitled *Band Aid 20: Justice, Not Charity*, which went behind the scenes of the recording and was broadcast by BBC1 on December 6. In *The Observer*, Laura Lee Davies saw the record as a triumph for Girl Power, seeing it as an almost all-girl event and focusing on the inclusion in the band of Dido, former S Club 7 girl Rachel Stevens, soul singer Beverley Knight, urban artistes such as Ms Dynamite and Jamelia, and blue-eyed soul girl Joss Stone. But for lovers of edgy grime and true street music, the greatest achievement of Band Aid 20, apart of course from the money it raised for charity, was getting Dizzee Rascal to the top of the charts just in time for Christmas. It was certainly a momentous occasion for Dizzee.

"Well, it was my first number one, so obviously a big moment," he said when asked by DMC World what it was like working on such a historic recording as 'Do They Know It's Christmas?'. "Chris Martin, Bono, Joss Stone and the rest of the group all around me, surreal. But to be honest, I was in and out of the studio quick time."

Dizzee was going mainstream, and branching out in ways that would have seemed unimaginable two years earlier. In 2004, he did an international endorsement deal with American urban clothing company Eckó, and designed his own shoe for Nike the following year. The rapper signed up to help promote the popular outfitter, based in New Jersey, in a new advertising campaign. It was shot early in 2004, for its autumn/winter collection, part of Eckó's move to recruit exciting up-and-coming artists from Europe. A clearly excited Dizzee, delighted that British fashion was being recognised in its own right after years of dominance by US hip hop fashion, told website Allhiphop.com: "England, we are coming up. Sometimes, though, people emulate what's coming from the United

States. There aren't that many people in London doing anything original." He was especially pleased to be providing an alternative to "bling-y" ostentation, with a truer representation of inner-London street style: "There was a time where people were dressing up with the champagne and all that bullshit, but niggas like me had hats, hoods, making our own beats, doing our own shit, and making our own way."

Whatever hat'n'hood ensemble Dizzee had been rocking, it was enough to convince his legions of fans that this was a look they had to have, while fashion brands could see the value of having such an edgy character from the notoriously incendiary garage and grime scenes fronting their products. It was Dizzee's style, a thrown-together melange of high street UK brands and US names such as American Apparel, of sportswear, baggy hoodies, baseball caps and trainers, especially Nike ones, that inevitably led to a collaboration with the footwear company. In 2005, Dizzee's hip hop cachet had reached the point where he had his very own personalised Nike Air 180s made exclusively for him, with his name on the back of each chunky trainer and a lovely Dirtee Stank logo – complete with a steaming mound of faeces and buzzing flies – on each of the shoe's tongues.

It wouldn't be his last tie-in with the iconic sports manufacturer: in 2009, Dizzee teamed up with British artist Ben Drury – responsible for the artwork for Dizzee's next album, 2007's *Maths + English*, as well as the 2009 follow-up, *Tongue N' Cheek* – to create the limited-edition Tongue N' Cheek Air Max 90. Launched a week ahead of the *Tongue N' Cheek* album at Nike's 1948 store in Shoreditch, east London, there was a small, exclusive number made, and all proceeds went to Tower Hamlets' Summer University where Dizzee had studied music several years before (see Chapter 2). Dizzee said of his latest venture: "The Air Max 90 is pretty much the street shoe, 'innit? It's quite sporty, but when you get the right colours you can wear it with anything. But with this one we tried to keep it quite plain so it could complete any outfit. It's functional and there was a pretty deep design process involved."

The Purple Revolver website took a more negative view in September 2009, when it reported that sportswear experts believed the Dizzee Rascal trainer would "start a sneaker war among avid collectors and fans" at the trendy 1948 shoe emporium. There were, said the website, scenes of "mad excitement" in New York and LA when limited-edition shoes were released via specialist stores, with "sneaker freaks camping out for days before they're released". It stated that, when only 30 Nike Pigeon Dunks went on sale at The Reed Space in NYC, "riot squads had to be called in to stop fighting and gangs stealing the shoes when buyers leave the premises". It also noted Dizzee's penchant for name-checking his favourite Nikes in his music, such as the lyric to 'Bubbles' on *Maths + English*, which went: "Nike Air Bubbles on my feet, looking fresh/Got my brand new garms on, dressed to impress." Purple Revolver, under the banner headline 'Dizzee Rascal To Cause Sneaker Pimp Wars', fully expected trouble when the limited-edition shoe hit the streets. "Sneaker collecting has become a multi-billion dollar global business and there are millions of collectors just buying up boxes of shoes to store as an investment," they wrote. "The shoes often go for triple their price on eBay within hours and Nike know what they are doing with the limited release in London. Given that Dizzee is Britain's first hip hop superstar, there is going to be a huge clamour for his shoes. Fans across the world are going to want a pair at any cost. We expect trouble to start outside the store. When the Nike Pigeon Dunk was released in Manhattan, there were kids sleeping outside in tents about four days before they went on sale. There were 150 collectors waiting for only 30 pairs. The cops made about 10–20 arrests. Gangs were waiting to steal them on the corner. After the crowd was cleared, they found machetes and baseball bats."

It is not known how furious the clamour was to get the shoe in the end; nevertheless, Dizzee's fashion star was undoubtedly in the ascendant. For the Style Icons For Him awards presented in 2009 by online magazine City Life, Dizzee was one of three male celebrities afforded the honour, alongside footballer David Beckham and *High School Musical* teen sensation Zac Efron. "As his status as a true inspiration to young Brits increases, young men across the country are keen to get the same look, particularly in London suburbs," the webzine declared. "Musicians have always influenced their fans' image to some extent, but Dizzee's style is more of a way of life for thousands of young men. Dizzee's made a real name for himself. His sense of style is just another reason why people love him."

And so it continued in 2010, when Dizzee's popularity in the charts made him an almost ubiquitous presence, as well as an urban style icon. Fashion website Handbag reported that London store Selfridges had enlisted the creative talents of "10 of music's hottest acts" for a unique new project called Sounds Of The Mind. Alongside some of the coolest names in pop – Paloma Faith, Charlotte Gainsbourg, Hot Chip, Florence And The Machine, Empire Of The Sun, The Drums, The XX, Marina And The Diamonds and The Big Pink – Dizzee was invited to create his very own window display based on one of his own songs, to be showcased at the store near London's Marble Arch from May 10 to the end of June as part of Selfridges' Music in May season.

He talked about his fashion favourites in DMC World. The online magazine asked him who he considered to be the best fashion designer of the moment and he replied: "A Gucci suit is still my number one," adding that he had just been to the awards ceremony for women's style bible *Glamour* and that it was "nice to see Kanye West, Adele and Estelle picking up awards", offering some idea of whom he regarded as cool contemporary style icons.

Dizzee Rascal, fashion maven? Had he sold out completely? It was around this time that Dizzee – who in his lyrics had expressed his "keeping it real" credentials but in interviews never made a secret of the fact that he had no intention of remaining a local sensation, appealing to grime purists only – hit out at critics who accused him of watering down his appeal for mass consumption and brand identification. He told *The Daily Star*: "People say I'm selling out but it doesn't get to me any more. It depends on what people mean by selling out, and who's saying it. Some people think it's morally wrong of me to not 'keep it real' but a lot of the time this is coming from drug dealers and robbers." He went on: "Does 'keeping it real' mean I have to stay underground, playing shit raves and chasing promoters for my money, when I can do a big pop show where they like me, look after me and pay me well? Some people think they've got ownership on me when they've never met me. My only job is to deliver what I think is inspiring and makes them move. While I'm so commercial, there's no point trying to prove how hard or underground I am. I might as well just keep it rolling. I know how to make edgy music, I enjoy that, but I'm going with what feels natural at this point. It's spreading joy. Everyone's in a good mood."

In spreading the word around the world, Dizzee was in danger of spreading himself too thin. During his US tour with The Streets back in 2004 – when his mission, along with DJ Slimzee from Pay As U Go Cartel on turntables, was to "bring LDN to the NYC!" – he had encountered a journalist from *Blender* magazine. The latter found him looking distinctly weary from jet-lag. But then, as he explained, he'd looked that way for years. "My body clock is effed," he said. "It has been for about three years. I don't know when I'm supposed to sleep." Nevertheless, he was delighted to discover that word about him – this time not as a fashion leader but as a musical innovator – had reached one of his all-time heroes: Keith Alam, alias Guru of Brooklyn hip hop pioneers Gang Starr. The rapper, who died in April 2010 aged 43, had been astonished by Dizzee's idiosyncratic but highly original vision. "That's like ragga mixed with hip hop with an incredible, original UK style," he enthused. "I honestly believe he can sell mad records in the States. He's got good energy, man." Dizzee could barely believe the accolade. "Coming from Guru? The essence of old-school hip hop? The real innovator? He's a pioneer."

It was while in the States that Dizzee found another home for his Dirtee Stank logo when he commissioned a jumpsuit with a spray-painted portrait on the front, plus his fly/faeces label logo. His manager and co-producer, Nick Cage, visited JMartin Designs on Melrose Avenue in Los Angeles with Dizzee. There, the owner, J Martin himself, custom-painted clothing for rappers Method Man and Xzibit, as well as for Jennifer Lopez and David Beckham. Cage apparently called over to his charge to find out what colour he wanted his jumpsuit to be: "Hey, Dizzee – you want the dog shit brown or white?"

It was also during that early US sojourn that Dizzee discovered how ubiquity could lead to overexposure – literally. While in LA, he was booked to appear on chat show *Jimmy Kimmel Live* for his American TV début. During rehearsals, the show's floor manager approached the rapper and warned him that he was revealing several inches of backside, which was deemed too much for American network television. Five minutes before Dizzee was due to appear live, Kimmel showed the audience a still from the rehearsal: that self-same expanse of exposed backside, only pixellated for a joke. Following a fabulously energetic performance of 'Fix Up, Look Sharp', Dizzee was nonchalant when reminded that a considerable section of his bare posterior might have been broadcast to an even more considerable section of the American nation. "Everything comes with a price," he said, looking around for a drink. Besides, as he added, quite straight-faced, "I thought my arse was blacker than that."

CHAPTER 11

Suk My Dick

"I've been on the edge of society. I've been looked at from a negative perspective most of my life. And that's not an exaggeration – that's real. [But] I ain't worried about being misunderstood, by any means."
                                                                Dizzee Rascal

There were a few prevailing images of Dizzee Rascal, and a couple of perceptions about who and what he was at both ends of the scale, at this mid-point in his career (taking 2001 as roughly the start and summer 2010, the time of writing this book, as the present): there was Dizzee the sonic innovator, and Dizzee the social agitator, as likely to make a name for himself via his lyrics as he was for his extracurricular activities.

As he told Garry Mulholland in *The Independent*, music was his escape from the world of violence and an alternative future as a miscreant. "And a lot more," he said. "'Cos over the last few years I ain't been short of people dying, getting shot and stabbed. The other day a friend got shot twice. That was always near me: fighting, bullshit, drugs, car crashes, crimes. Not that I'm the biggest hardened criminal in the world. I got caught up and whatever." He explained that, from his début single 'I Luv U' onwards, he had finally found an outlet for his frustrations, feelings that might otherwise have got him into trouble. "With 'I Luv U', it was, 'At last – another place to go, aside from home.'"

He continued, alluding to the 2003 near-fatal Ayia Napa incident (see Chapter 6) but talking generally about the sort of company he tended to keep: "Shit happens, can I say that in your paper? This isn't new to me. I've been in a few life-threatening situations. It sounds so clichéd that I don't even wanna say it." He admitted that he dearly wanted to alter the perception of himself as the delinquent east Londoner, but worried that it was too late. "I don't know if I can end the image, y'know?" he said, sadly, adding: "But what's important is that I'm alive and I'm here."

Mulholland intimated that it might not be possible to have one without the other: that, in order to create edgy music, you need to be living on the edge yourself. In order for Dizzee to be able to absorb the sounds of the multicultural city, from "the bhangra or dancehall reggae coming from a car" to "the constant trebly chirp of mobile ringtones and car alarms", it was necessary for him to truly immerse himself in the capital, and if that meant being exposed to some of the more negative aspects of London life, then so be it. That was the price, as he saw it, of telling the truth about 21st century inner-city Britain, about "the constant conflict and stress of ghetto life" with its "blend of struggle, violence and hustling to survive". As a result, he found himself frequently misunderstood, not to mention rather negatively perceived. Complained Dizzee: "Listen, man... I've been on the edge of society. Misunderstood? Misunderstood? Young, black, misunderstood... I've been looked at from a negative perspective most of my life. And that's not an exaggeration – that's real. That's what people expect me to say, but I still will and I'm not scared of saying it. So I ain't worried about being misunderstood, by any means."

Those misunderstandings continued when, in March 2005, Dizzee was arrested after being caught allegedly carrying pepper spray, classified as an illegal firearm in the UK. The "suspicious vehicle" he was travelling in, as a passenger, was stopped by police in east London on March 2, 2005 and, according to the BBC, he was arrested. A police spokesperson announced that he had been taken into custody at an east London police station and he was later released on bail, to return on April 8.

Unfortunately, Dizzee had a show in America – in Salt Lake City, Utah – scheduled for the day he was due to report to the police station to answer bail. Nevertheless, he did go ahead with his spring 2005 US dates, designed to promote his second album, *Showtime*, and further spread the word about grime in the States. Not that he skipped bail or refused to submit to follow any procedure, just that the charges were presumably dropped because nothing further was heard of the incident. On March 31, he performed at the Doug Fir Lounge in Portland, Oregon, where journalist Gray Gannaway reported excitedly on the "poster boy for a new hybrid of electronic hip hop called 'grime'". Gannaway found a club packed full of ardent Dizzee-philes, most of whom could "sing Rascal's songs word for word, an amazing feat in itself given Dizzee's thick British accent and rapid-fire flow." Along with Dizzee's rapping partner Scope, and with DJ Wonder on the decks, Gannaway concluded that, "As great as Dizzee's albums are, his live show is even more mesmerising".

Dizzee himself confirmed that, live, he was all about action and power. "People will be surprised at the energy," he said. "It's just me, a DJ, and a hypeman. It's not a lot of set-up on stage but I'm good at it. Bring the shit to life a lot; I think people get it more at the show, even if they already have the album." He admitted that he found American audiences to be "more bubbly" than English ones, whom he considered "quite cold". In the States, he said, "People are not afraid to wild out and have a good time."

Dizzee was interviewed during the US tour by a newspaper in Houston, for an article that made connections between the grime music of the day, with its roots in London's underclass, and the Seventies hip hop of the Bronx, the Eighties hip hop of LA's Compton district and the contemporary rap emanating from Houston's own Fifth Ward district. "Poverty knows no national boundaries," ran the article. "It looks similar everywhere you go: broken glass, discarded syringes and filthy government housing are just part of the ghetto-universal template." It described Dizzee, because of the pepper-spray incident of the previous month, as a "fugitive from justice", while using his April 14 gig at the city's Engine Room venue as an opportunity to celebrate grime as the London equivalent of New York hip hop and Brazil's favela funk. The writer described grime as "a sonic revelation" and "one of the most compelling sounds of the new millennium", with its "bubbling bass, breakneck, drum'n'bass-inspired rhythms, and dirty and at times convoluted samples", going on to favourably compare it with the raw urgency of early hip hop. "Its emcees," he added, "come equipped with thick Cockney accents [who] spit in frantic flows that owe equal parts to ragga toasting and crunk's hollered, rushed rhythms."

But it was the innovator/agitator dialectic that marked Dizzee out as special. "I came straight from the pirate radio scene, straight from the streets," he said. "That's an important part of mine and a lot of other people's past." Some American journalists, noting his desire to escape his street hustler past yet acknowledging his violent, desperate background, compared him to literate, poetic US rapper Nas. And although some made light of Dizzee's recent arrest for offences that, stacked up against the Uzi and Glock-wielding US hip hoppers, seemed relatively slight, Dizzee – along with other up-and-coming grime artists such as Lady Sovereign and Kano, who back then looked set to break in the States – was being regarded as the avatar for a generation of young, poor and politically powerless minorities, even if the man himself was concerned that the violence of the grime scene was overshadowing its pioneering musical aspect. "They [the media] overlook that this is a self-sustaining scene that came from inner-city London, that came from nothing and is now being recognised on an international level," he said.

American journalists were fascinated by the furore caused by grime in the UK and the way even politicians had weighed angrily into the debate about the music's supposed pernicious influence on young people. Dizzee blamed the media for making grime a scapegoat. "They've turned it into something else," he said. Indeed, it hadn't been long since then-Home Secretary David Blunkett and former Culture Minister Kim Howells had famously blamed rap for "glorifying gun culture and violence". In 2003, Blunkett had railed against rap's "appalling" lyrics, while Howells issued a statement attacking grime artists for helping to create a culture "where killing is almost a fashion accessory" and made comments that many grime supporters regarded as racist, especially when he denigrated rappers and grime crews as a bunch of "boasting macho idiot rappers". In the dock for the defence was ex-*NME* editor Conor McNicholas (later the editor of car magazine *Top Gear*), who responded to Howells' inflammatory claims by saying: "He doesn't understand the culture. It is this idea again that we have to do something about these out-of-control black people in our streets and the nasty culture they are perpetuating. They are deeply racist sentiments. We have to be absolutely clear: the gun culture is a function of urban deprivation and not because of the music. The music reflects the experience of young people and doesn't create it. There is more rap music listened to and bought by white kids in Swindon than there is by black kids in Hackney, and nobody is talking about the gun culture on the streets of white suburban Britain." McNicholas proposed that Howells knew little of the subject and suggested he stick to matters with which he was more familiar. "He clearly doesn't know what he is talking about. We have to recognise that these are young kids who are growing up in very difficult environments who happen to make music as a way of expressing themselves and their frustrations. Just because these guys are making music about the situation they are in does not mean they are perpetuating the culture. The music is not creating the problem."

Not everyone was obsessed with the social subtext of Dizzee Rascal's music – many just enjoyed the noise. In April 2005, in an interview with US webzine Pop Matters, the journalist encountered an intelligent, engaged and engaging young man, whose current reading matter was *The Hitchhiker's Guide to the Galaxy* ("a fucked-up book"), and who enjoyed talking extensively about his musical influences. His all-time favourite rap artist was, he said, Jay-Z, whom he supported live in concert at Wembley when he was just 17. "I don't think hip hop or music has seen anything like him ever," he said. But it was Tupac Shakur and Bone Thugs-N-Harmony who had been his initiation into the joys of hip hop as a boy, while drum'n'bass, rave and techno had been the other soundtrack to his youth.

Thereafter, he explained, he discovered everything from crunk to grunge and metal – he loved Guns N' Roses, Metallica and Nirvana. But it was Jay-Z who got him most excited, especially the US rapper's legendary gift for improvising in the studio. Asked whether he had similar skills, he replied: "Yeeeeah. Wicked! Sometimes it can be like that ... I might've written a load of stuff and just recited it, so it's in my head. Sometimes I might go to the studio and there's a beat and I could find something to just go with it quickly, rap and freestyle. Other times I just might have to live with the music, live with the beat for a bit. I might have to take it home and live with it or rap it down in the studio, whether I made it or whether someone else produced it."

Of more recent artists, he cited production overlords the Neptunes and Timbaland and "Dirty South" funk-rappers OutKast as examples of artists with whom he dreamed of collaborating in the future. He liked the Neptunes' playful approach to production, particularly on their track 'Drop It Like It's Hot'. "Mmmm..." he seemed to gasp with pleasure. "That beat's very naughty. They take the piss, they're very important."

He also discussed his development as an MC, putting his prowess down to sheer practice via live performance and pirate radio: "Even before the record deal, I kind of came up doing a lot of live stuff as well as pirate radio... so I'd be on for two hours at a time and singing straight, doing clubs and raves." Finally, he reminisced about his days entering contests as a battling rhymer, which he didn't really miss: "I never really liked it," he said. "I did it, yeah. I can't ever say I lost, but after a while it all comes out a waste of time. It's all good, but I enjoy entertaining through a song. I get more kicks out of that."

Not too much was heard of Dizzee between spring 2005 and spring 2006. Along with The Bravery and Supergrass he was confirmed as one of the artists for a new London-wide music festival called Bud Rising, which would see established acts headlining on a bill of acts that they would pick themselves, while newer artists would have an opportunity to perform, in a series of free "rising" gigs, at smaller venues in the city. In May 2005 it was announced that Dizzee was to properly launch – or rather, relaunch – his own record label, Dirtee Stank, and use it as an opportunity to discover new talent and release their music, even though the imprint was first employed back in 2002 for the original white-label 12-inch release of his début single, 'I Luv U'.

Dirtee Stank (the name – US slang for pungent – was the antithesis of all things shiny and bling), stated Dizzee and co-runner Nick Cage would be an alternative to major labels who "try to dilute the music". The first signings were Leicester rap trio Klass A, said to be "the first crew outside of London to really push the social boundaries of grime", and Newham Generals, aka D Double E, Footsie and Monkey, who hailed from east London and were apparently "the hottest live act on the road". Footsie explained: "What's unique about Dirtee Stank is that it's not run by people who are out of touch, who don't know what's going on or what we're experiencing. It's being run by people who are still doing it. Dizzee's still doing it – he's in touch with the scene and [that's why] we've been brought in."

Dizzee corroborated this later on when, in the wake of further successes in the charts, he said: "We'll be signing the most exciting street talent the UK has to offer. We add a pinch of both worlds. I have an understanding as to what it's like to be in the mainstream. And obviously I'm from the street. I did the whole underground thing and was one of the pioneers when it comes to grime. We were the first to be selling thousands of white labels so I can definitely bridge the gap and make big things happen, man." He told Dave Simpson of *The Guardian*: "Before I got a record deal, before I was on pirate radio or anything, I used to make tapes and have MCs come around for the fun of it. [Running Dirtee Stank] feels like going back to that. I like the idea of finding good music and showing it to the world." Added Cage, who was according to Dizzee the Angelo Dundee to his Muhammad Ali: "As ever, the majors are jumping on the wrong things and consequently stemming the possibilities for other artists." As a result, he said, "There's a massive gap between what you would call an underground label and a major record label. We're trying to find a way to bridge that gap."

Dizzee intended to involve his signings – some grime, others on the broader urban spectrum – on the soundtrack to a movie he was involved in called *Rollin' With The Nines*, about a rap group turned drug-dealing cartel, then in post-production. "It's the first black British gangster film, like *Snatch* or one of those – but a bit more serious," said Dizzee, who had a small acting role in the film as a crack dealer.

As though to prove his adaptability and rising status as the figurehead of a generation, on Wednesday May 10 the following year Dizzee was invited to speak as well as perform at the Oxford Union, where characters of the magnitude and gravitas of Ronald Reagan, Richard Nixon, Yasser Arafat and Pervez Musharraf (and Michael Winner) had previously made historic appearances. During the evening at the University, he spoke about his life, his career and his plans for the future, and followed this up by performing a selection of tracks, including previews of material from his next album, the follow-up to 2004's *Showtime*, due to be titled *Maths + English*.

Hilarious footage of the night's events soon appeared on YouTube, including Dizzee wowing the decidedly uncomfortable-looking Annabelles and Jeremys in the audience with his rendition of 'Fix Up, Look Sharp' ahead of his speech, which partly inspired Oliver Burkeman of *The Guardian* to pen an article accusing the Union of being out of touch. "For a demonstration of the awkwardness its members have sometimes displayed in trying to adapt to the 21st century, readers with a taste for *schadenfreude* are invited to search YouTube for clips of the hip hop artist Dizzee Rascal performing there live last year," he wrote in an article entitled "Why Does Anyone Care About The Oxford Union?"

Just as the students of Oxford were being educated about Dizzee, the rapper was about to give some more lessons of his own, namely in *Maths + English*.

CHAPTER 12

Wanna Be

"I want that Beatles shit. I wanna see that Snoop Dogg status – them kind of levels, international. It will take some grind but I'm down for it. What else is there to do? I might as well."

Dizzee Rascal

Before Dizzee Rascal could prove he had what it took to make a storming third album, there was a period of consolidation. During the middle of the Noughties, there was further evidence of the inroads he had made into the mainstream, and of his crossover status, when it was confirmed that he would be appearing at the Carling Weekend Reading and Leeds festivals, not normally a haven for rappers (indeed, when his hero, Jay-Z, performed at Glastonbury two years later it caused a furore), at the end of summer 2006. Despite headlining on the *NME* stage at the same time that the then–popular indie band Kaiser Chiefs were headlining on the main stage, Dizzee drew a big crowd and entertained allcomers with a high energy set. He also played to massive audiences that summer when he toured Europe with American rock band Red Hot Chili Peppers, whom Dizzee deemed "cool as fuck". He used the opportunity, he said, to "try and understand the power and intensity music's got to have to get across to people in that situation".

He didn't have much of an audience in September 2006, however, when he performed – for a free music event staged by T-Mobile – in front of a far smaller crowd at a venue beneath London Bridge in south-east London called the Vaults. There were only a few hundred fans (who got in after emailing their mobile numbers) present that night, although thanks to the theatre company Shunt, who brought along all manner of stilt walkers and conjurors for the occasion, there was a lively carnivalesque atmosphere.

Not that Dizzee's performance involved such gimmickry. As journalist Andre Paine reported, it was a stripped-down affair, the rapper joined onstage by another MC and his DJ. Dizzee focused instead on his trademark artillery-fire vocals and mixed up favourites from his two albums with teasers from his long-awaited third. He opened with 'Jus' A Rascal' and closed with 'Stand Up Tall'; in between, there were snippets from the DJ of Queen's 'Another One Bites The Dust' and Gnarls Barkley's 'Crazy', alongside new tracks 'Flex' (which saw him accompanied onstage by a couple of gyrating girls in pink underwear and blonde wigs), 'Sirens', 'Da Feelin'' – "an exhilarating combination of drum'n'bass and Jamaican dancehall", according to Paine, which featured a sample of blue-eyed soul girl Joss Stone's voice – and "dreary marijuana anthem" 'Lemon' (which eventually got cut from the forthcoming album, *Maths + English*). Paine concluded of the gig that "Dizzee earned his cheque", although he added that he couldn't quite bring himself to applaud the mobile phone company that had staged the event, in spite of the rapper's attempts to get the audience to do just that.

London Bridge aside, Dizzee had come a long way from Bow. He spent much of the mid-Noughties travelling far from his birthplace in east London. He went to Argentina, Chile and Brazil and spent a lot of time touring America, where he performed in Los Angeles, New York, Philadelphia, Washington, Chicago, Portland, Oregon, San Francisco and Texas among other places. But it all felt more like business than pleasure. "It's definitely work," he said. "I take it very seriously. My eye's always on the ball. The fun part is being on stage. That's when you can let loose. Everything else you have to keep your eye on. If you don't treat it like work, like it's not a business, you slip up. I'm a music lover, but I'm in the music business. It's two different things almost."

Chances to chill out were, he explained in a lengthy and revealing interview in early 2006 with the writer of the dubstep and grime blog Blackdown, few and far between. This was due to promotional duties and the constant demands of networking, even at clubs on nights off. "It don't really stop, but at the same time do you want it to?" he asked, aware that music careers these days can be short-lived. "It'll stop if you want it. Then you'll be that person who used to be famous who everyone still recognises but you're broke."

He found he was manageably famous in the States. "It's not pandemonium," he said. "It's overwhelming sometimes because you're that far away. You have to check yourself, like, 'You serious?' Being famous… I can't fathom it myself really." Fame, he admitted, was a burden, but nothing he couldn't handle. "You get over it, you know the people like your music and what you're doing. That's what it's about." Nor was he troubled by the increasing perception of him as a mainstream artist. "The whole thing of me being mainstream, it hasn't stunted my growth. But it's shown people I still know where I'm from – it's a part of me, so whether I'm doing it physically myself or introducing it myself, people still get to hear it and understand." It would be easy, he accepted, to allow the extracurricular pursuits and accoutrements of celebrity to go to his head – "the money, the girls, the champagne", as he put it – but he always kept his focus. "I've always got my eye on the ball. And I've got a real genuine love for the music. It's easy to get caught up in all the extra shit. I don't knock it, but it's easy for it to become the sole purpose of why you do it."

That was the joy of playing live – the crowd response was all the buzz he really needed; seeing people appreciate his music. "I like getting paid but I like seeing 10,000 people jumping up and down, happy; 10,000 people who don't know each other necessarily, coming to the same place to jump around, to bubble to what you have, and forget all their bullshit for an hour or sumthin'. Forget all the bullshit in the world for an hour and bubble." It was this, after all, more than the financial remuneration, that initially drove him to want to become a recording and performing artist. "It weren't money that drove me to do it in the first place. Music was my love. [At first] it was a sideline thing, but then I took it serious, more serious than what I was doing. Thank god for that."

Having supported Jay-Z at Wembley in front of 35,000 people (he'd also opened for many other peers and heroes, including Pharrell Williams, Nas, R&B pop lothario Justin Timberlake and reggae artist Sean Paul), and performed before even more at the V and Reading festivals, there was, he decided, "never a crowd too big". He joked about being as big as the Fab Four – "I want that Beatles shit" – or the biggest rapper of them all. "I wanna see that Snoop Dogg status," he said, "them kind of levels, international. It will take some grind but I'm down for it. What else is there to do? I might as well. The Pope knows Snoop. The Queen knows Snoop Dogg. Everyone knows Snoop Dogg, household name." He even relished the prospect of being mobbed in the street by marauding teenagers, which was just as well considering the level of fame that he would enjoy by the end of the decade. "Yeah, man, fuckin' give it to me, if I'm making more people happy with it," he said. The only obstacle to overcome, he concluded, was ensuring that his music retained its essential edgy quality and link to the streets that made him what he was. He said it was important to experiment, to try new things and adopt different approaches. "Just stretch yourself," he said. "I always look inside myself and think, 'Right, I've done that, lemme try and go that way.' Go as far and deep inside yourself as you can. I'm always looking for that, so that's where the range comes from, the variety."

One sensed that, after the relatively disappointing *Showtime*, which found him lyrically defensive and musically treading water after the ground-breaking *Boy In Da Corner*, Dizzee had rediscovered his mojo following two years out of the recording studio and fairly constant performing. By summer 2007, energised by the direct reaction he'd been getting from audiences around the world, he seemed to be brimming with confidence. On June 7, Dizzee came on late to play a short, two-song set for the Proud Galleries' Another Music = Another Kitchen night in Camden, north London. Despite its brevity, it was, according to the reviewer from London listings magazine *Time Out*, an exuberant show, the crowd "ecstatic" at their proximity to Dizzee, who proclaimed himself, in a fit of hubris, "the biggest selling artist in UK rap history". It was, noted the reviewer, a mainly white, 'indie' crowd, which didn't faze Dizzee one iota ("I'm used to playing in front of indie crowds," he said later). Nor was he unsettled by the over-the-top response to his set. "My fans are lunatics," he laughed. "I encourage mosh pits, I encourage lunacy, I make music to let go to. When I started, I was making music for the hood, but even back then I was still always into broadening out, into making music for everyone. I've accepted them as part of my fan base."

Dizzee toured the length and breadth of Britain, from Edinburgh to Plymouth, on his Dirtee Stank tour throughout spring and summer 2007. Inevitably, it was the London shows that drew the most music reviewers. At Koko, also in Camden, Dizzee was in equally explosive form, according to the *Evening Standard*, which described it as an "electrifying show", going on to report that, "Dizzee Rascal did more than enough to confirm his status as London's number one rapper." He showcased material from the third album, Dizzee apparently demonstrating "not only his unwavering technical tightness and showmanship but also the fact that his latest compositions represent a natural progression from his previous work." Dressed in white cap and Dirtee Stank T-shirt, which he soon whipped off to reveal an impressive washboard stomach, Dizzee, wrote the *Standard*, "revealed that his body, like his music, has become leaner and stronger".

Rahul Verma of *The Independent* was at the same gig and was equally full of praise. Dizzee put "more energy and effort into the first five minutes than you usually see in an entire hip hop concert", and was "utterly at ease in the spotlight, prowling, dancing, shadow-boxing and surveying the crowd". After an incendiary 'Fix Up, Look Sharp', DJ Semtex introduced Fat Joe's 2004 anthem 'Lean Back', after which there was an encore, for which Dizzee was joined by Dirtee Stank label signings Newham Generals for a track aimed at "the smokers" – a cover of 'Puff The Magic Dragon'. By the end of the gig, the "sweating, breathless audience" were baying for more and Dizzee had proved his ability to transform a regular gig into a full-blown rave. Wrote Verma: "Dizzee's grasp of gig dynamics is as thrilling and impressive as his music."

His track record was assured – or at least, he had a landmark début album under his belt, if not a particularly strong follow-up. The gap between those first two albums had been short, with just a year separating them. As the years passed – 2005, then 2006 – critics and fans began to wonder when new material would be forthcoming. Speaking to Blackdown in February 2006, he explained that he had "put a couple of music ideas down", even if he hadn't really completed anything in full, although he did have a title for the album – *Maths + English* – as well as a game plan. "I'm just trying to do things that I haven't done before, again," he promised. "Trying to widen, reach the masses a bit more. Try and make the best music I can."

He had already recorded "a few bits" with Newham Generals, fellow Dirtee Stank signees Klass A, east London producer/DJ Mizz Beats and drum'n'bass legend Andre Williams, alias Shy FX. "The drum'n'bass influence will always be there," said Dizzee of *Maths + English*, adding, "I can't wait for the album to be done." Whatever the ultimate direction of the album, it would, guaranteed Dizzee, be equally experimental and accessible, and it would be a from-the-heart account of where he was at, musically and lyrically. He dreamed of ascending to that select pantheon of icons like Marvin Gaye and Snoop Dogg, artists who over a long period made music that was honest and true, yet still hugely popular. "They've reached people because they mean it and they've established themselves," he said. "I'm on that." When asked by Blackdown which of his two albums so far he preferred, he hedged his bets and replied, "It changes," adding that, for him, listening to his own work was exactly that – work. It was an arduous process, simply because he had heard the songs so many times and was at the point where he would analyse every last note, unable to ignore the imperfections. This, in turn, created another dilemma – having to be sufficiently thick-skinned to withstand the criticisms levelled at music that had, as he put it, "really come from inside". As a consequence, unlike those musicians who feigned indifference when it came to reactions to their work, Dizzee was sensitive to criticism, especially considering his music was aimed at reaching the masses as much as it was designed to please himself. "I do care how people perceive it," he said. "Definite."

The first news about the much-anticipated new album had appeared in April 2007, when the title *Maths + English* was revealed and the release date set – June 4, when it would be competing with new albums from Paul McCartney, Bruce Springsteen, shock-rocker Marilyn Manson and R&B songbird Rihanna. It was to be preceded by a single, 'Sirens', on May 21. The album would include a collaboration with Sheffield indie band Arctic Monkeys (Dizzee had recently appeared on their song 'Temptation Greets You Like Your Naughty Friend', one of the tracks on the band's April 2007 'Brianstorm' EP). It would also feature singer Lily Allen on the track 'Wanna Be', rapper UGK on 'Where Da G's' and Newham Generals on 'Lemon' (although the latter was subsequently dropped from the album). Production contributions would come from the likes of Nick Cage and Shy FX, while other tracks set to appear on the album were 'Pussyole', 'Industry', 'Flex' and 'Bubbles'. The decision was taken in May 2007 to release the album only digitally in the States in June, perhaps because of the disappointing sales there of *Showtime*. It had also been reported that Dizzee was reluctant to promote the new album on the other side of the Atlantic, although that was unlikely given his enthusiasm for touring there.

Anticipation surrounding *Maths + English* was heightened by the broadcast, at midnight on Sunday June 3, mere hours before the album's appearance in the shops, of a Channel 4 documentary about the making of the record, entitled *Bow Selector*. Advance publicity from record company XL about the documentary was terse but tantalising: "If all you know about Dizzee Rascal is his 2003 Mercury Music Prize, then this is essential viewing," went the advert, emblazoned with early reactions from the media to Dizzee's third album. "Has Dizzee made the best UK hip hop album ever?" went the quote from *Observer Music Monthly*, sounding more like a statement than a question. Then there was some explanation on the advert as to the content of the documentary, which was directed by Goetz Werner (who directed the video to Dizzee's single 'Graftin"), with Nick Cage as executive producer: "Dizzee talks about his musical journey so far," it said, adding that there would be cameo appearances from "a rapping Jonathan Ross", collaborator and fan Lily Allen, US R&B-rockers N★E★R★D, a cartoon narrated by former Happy Mondays bug-eyed dancing loon Bez, "and much more".

Bow Selector followed Dizzee's rise from unsigned hopeful to Mercury Prize winner and beyond, with successes at home and abroad. It showed him talking from his studio, which some viewers found engaging and interesting, while others considered him in these segments overly brash. There were clips of him performing live with Pharrell Williams' N★E★R★D, and a series of fun comic shorts, narrated by Bez, called "Everybody Hates Dizz", portraying Dizzee growing up (the title of the shorts was a pun on US comedian Chris Rock's sitcom about growing up in the Eighties, *Everybody Hates Chris*). In addition, the film contained footage of Dizzee's début as a speaker at the Oxford University Union and Dizzee's young cousin. Perhaps the most memorable section of *Bow Selector* was his brief encounter with Jonathan Ross, in which Britain's pre-eminent chat show host was encouraged to rap the verse from Dizzee's *Showtime* intro: "Inside, outside, rah rah rah..."

"He's a cheeky bastard," Dizzee told Ben Thompson *of Observer Music Monthly* with a grin. "I wanted to hear him saying 'wah wah wah' because he has trouble with his r's'."

Dizzee really was now ready to give his lesson in *Maths + English*.

CHAPTER 13

Curriculum Vital

"I've done a lot of it and if I do say myself it's banging. Quote me on that, please."

Dizzee Rascal on *Maths + English*

The first piece of music anyone heard from Dizzee Rascal's third album, *Maths + English*, was 'Sirens', which was released as a single on May 21, 2007, although he'd actually been performing the song live for quite a while. His seventh single, 'Sirens', was featured on BBC Radio 1's 1-Upfront playlist and, despite less than overwhelming amounts of airplay, earnt him a Top 20 placing, his fourth such hit so far. It was also his first single to be released on seven-inch vinyl, backed by a track called 'Like Me' (the CD single came with another new song called 'Dean').

It augured well for the album. Featuring the sort of busy, bustling, dense, heavy sound collage not heard since the heyday of Public Enemy, and with the urban squall of NWA's classic 'Straight Outta Compton', 'Sirens' was a showcase for Dizzee and Nick Cage's production talents, recapturing as it did the glory days of the Bomb Squad and Dr Dre. Of course, this was Dizzee, straight outta

Hackney, so the rap may have been harrowing, but it was leavened with humour, full of parochial references to "burger and chips" and TV soap *EastEnders* and peppered with local slang ("bredder", "prang", etc). Nevertheless, 'Sirens' was as ghastly in its realism as its US hip hop counterparts, a dark evocation of street crime from the perspective of a vicious mugger.

A superb example of what Dizzee himself calls at the outset of the song "old school story-telling shit", it starts with half a dozen of Limehouse's finest constabulary knocking on his door at eight-thirty in the morning, arresting him on suspicion of a crime, having caught him on CCTV. Dizzee suspects that he's been shopped by one of his "pussy homeboys" and immediately worries that he will end up in jail – the air of intimidation is heightened by the sense that this had been a very real potential outcome of Dizzee's life had he not become a successful musician. The second verse recounts the mugging in grim detail as Dizzee and his henchmen, Aldo and Clayton, creep up on, then attack, a husband and wife holding hands walking home through an alleyway towards their flat. Even Dizzee the assailant is startled by the ferocity of his attack, calling it ruthless and tragic, as well as describing it as hellish. Despite being witnessed by an old schoolfriend, Aleesha, and facing a long period in prison, by the end of the song Dizzee remains unrepentant, refusing to change or divert from his law-breaking path. The final couplet represents as chilling a climax to a work of fiction as the final line of classic Thirties crime drama *I Am A Fugitive From A Chain Gang*, in which Paul Muni responds to the question, "How do you live?", with the words, "I steal!" before disappearing into the shadows.

The video to 'Sirens' had some of that Hollywood movie's neo-noir energy, even if it saw Dizzee assuming the role of the victim, not the perpetrator, of crime. It showed foxhunters on horses trampling down his front door, then chasing Dizzee, topless until he put on a jacket with a fur-trimmed hood (the symbolism was hardly subtle), through his flat and onto the cold, dark night-time streets. By the end of the video, he is trapped down an alleyway and savaged off-screen, his blood-streaked fur smeared by the hunters across their faces, a rictus of pleasure creeping across their cruel faces.

'Sirens' was, however, unrepresentative of the rest of *Maths + English*, which was produced and mixed by Dizzee Rascal, Nick Cage and Shy FX at Belly Of The Beast/Raskit's Lair studios, and released on June 4, 2007 (although in the States it remained unreleased until April 2008, where it was issued, on the Definitive Jux label, with two extra songs, 'G.H.E.T.T.O.' and 'Driving With Nowhere To Go', and minus the track 'Pussyole [Old Skool]'). *Maths + English* saw him finally wave goodbye to his 'ghetto' past and embrace the wider world. He talked in an interview before the album's release about the two words in the album's title.

"It's called *Maths + English* because that's what I do," he told online journal Left Lion. "Producing is all numbers, it's 'Maths'. And 'English', obviously, [is about] the writing, and where I'm from, England. It says it all, man."

He explained that he had been recording with Newham Generals' D Double E and Footsie, "for some production that's on more [of] that grimey take", as well as Shy FX. "I'm branching out, man, all over the place," he said, proudly. "There definitely is a vibe about it." He also talked about the progression from *Boy In Da Corner* through *Showtime* and onto the imminent third album. "I think I tried to go a bit deeper [on *Showtime*], technically as far as verses and stuff like that. I wanted to show deeper skills. The first one was a lot more hook-orientated and simple, but I wanted to make something different for the second. There was a lot of speculation as to whether I could do it again, the curse of the Mercury Prize and all sorts. Now I'm in the middle of the third. I've done a lot of it and if I do say myself it's banging. Quote me on that, please," he joked.

Dizzee had every right to sound confident. Everything about *Maths + English* felt bold, bright and confident. The vivid pink sleeve, courtesy of Ben Drury, signified a dramatic shift towards pop after the dour design for *Showtime*. The contributions of electronic musician Matthew Herbert on two tracks – on flute for 'Suk My Dick' and keyboards for 'Flex' – signalled a willingness to look beyond the confines of grime/garage, as did the appearance on 'Wanna Be' of Lily Allen's writing/production team Future Cut (credited as Futurecuts on the inner sleeve). Meanwhile, Mike Hedges (Manic Street Preachers, The Cure) proved a safe pair of hands when it came to mastering, giving the overall sound a clarity it might otherwise have lacked.

As soon as the first track, 'World Outside', began, it was apparent that Dizzee and Cage were newly energised and had returned to the form they had shown on the début album. It immediately sounded cleaner, crisper, as though there was a great big hole open to the titular world outside blasting fresh air through the recording studio. It started with a swirling, effects-laden (or Shy FX-laden) series of whooshing Oriental sounds, before Dizzee entered the fray, less highly strung this time round, his voice not the staccato yelp we'd grown accustomed to but a calmer, more measured affair. The poignant rap began with a paean to his manor, although there was a giant "but" coming as he effectively bid farewell to his council estate past and welcomed his new life as a successful recording artist and bona fide chart star. Not for him criminal misdemeanours anymore; he'd replaced all that with more fruitful antics in the recording studio. He may have been mired in crime in the past, but grime was affording him a bright future: over synth swooshes and whirls, he announced that he had moved away from "the hood" and the grime scene that proved his launch pad.

And that's how *Maths + English* proceeded – as a tour of musical styles that included virtually everything but straight grime, despite what he told Left Lion. 'Pussyole (Old Skool)' was old-school rap revisited, its sample from Lyn Collins' soul staple 'Think (About It)' (written by James Brown) adding to the late-Eighties hip hop feel. The character mentioned in the song, an older MC whom Dizzee used to look up to and soon came to regard with disdain as something of a fake, was rumoured to be former sparring partner Wiley, but even if it wasn't the track contained some blistering lines that came at the listener at warp speed (it is alleged that 'Letter 2 Dizzee', from Wiley's 2007 album *Playtime Is Over*, was penned as an attempt to end the rift between the pair, although it could hardly have been a response to 'Pussyole' because Wiley's album was released the exact same week as *Maths + English*). Even though it was a diatribe aimed at various haters, schemers and "shotters" (drug dealers), somehow, perhaps because of the sparky soundtrack, it lacked the spite and venom, the dragging bitterness and negativity, of *Showtime*.

After 'Sirens' came 'Where's Da G's', which featured Bun B and Pimp C of Texan hip hop duo UGK (Dizzee returned the favour when he appeared on the track 'Two Type Of Bitches' from UGK's 2007 album *Underground Kingz*). Slow, sparse and electronic, full of malice and menace, it still felt lighter than anything on *Showtime*, a feeling enhanced by the refrain and its attendant Dr Dre-ish trebly synth whine. With the two guest rappers – the first deep and gruff, the second whiny and high – 'Where's Da G's' came across like classic NWA, even as it called out the quintessential gangsta/playa/ pimp character, recognisable from rap lore, for being a fake and a poseur with a suggestion to said character not to wear his trousers so low.

'Paranoid' comprised more swirling sonics, but the attractive ambience was at odds with a song about anxiety and dread alleged to have been inspired by a real kidnap plot. As Dizzee told *Observer Music Monthly*, it was a gang, including former friends, who had made the bid to kidnap him when he started to enjoy chart success, believing they could demand a considerable ransom from his record company, XL, as a result. "When you start to make a bit of money, people switch on you," he said. "They get the wrong end of the stick. They think you're this or that, but really it's just that they miss you. And because of the kind of people they are, they don't deal with it properly: they can only respond with violence." Dizzee later played down rumours that he was the target of a plot, perhaps fearful that haters might be inspired to do exactly that. The 21-year-old claimed that he was never in any real danger, saying: "People you grew up with, some of them, that's just the type of thing that comes out of their mouth. There was no big kidnapping plot." Nevertheless, the music effectively comprised a paranoid soundscape as the lyrics portrayed him lying in bed alone at night, beleaguered, "a nervous wreck", going slowly insane as he imagined all manner of conspiracies and threats against him, trusting no one, from gold-digging girlfriends to so-called friends on his estate. By the end, he realised he had but one choice: to leave the unhealthy, claustrophobic environs of his home behind and find a newer, bigger space to roam. Short, snappy, sharp, incisive, 'Paranoid' was the polar opposite of his portentous previous album.

Next, 'Suk My Dick' came as light relief, with its references to kids' TV cartoons such as *Dangermouse*, its whistling refrain to 'Yankee Doodle Dandy' and rhyming of "mush" (as in "mouth") with "Georgy Bush". A song boldly proclaiming his indifference to criticisms that he was some kind of all-swearing antisocial nuisance, it posited Dizzee as a sort of latter-day, rap-age Johnny Rotten (his lyric and general tone of antipathy reverberated with memories of The Sex Pistols' "And we don't caaaare!"). And yet 'Suk My Dick' was no ponderous grind, it was tuneful and concise – indeed, there were only two tracks on *Maths + English* that ran over the four-minute mark. 'Flex' was faster, a nod to the 2step garage scene that birthed him, with lively little instrumental details to add to the sense of play – unlike the début album, which was fiercely inventive but featured music that contrasted with the lyrical fury, here Dizzee seemed to have fewer axes to grind and was simply relishing the freedom to create. 'Flex' found Dizzee on the pull, hoping the sexy girl in his sights didn't fancy another fella, and throwing caution to the wind. Continuing with his genre tourism, 'Da Feelin'' (Joss Stone was originally going to appear on the song but Dizzee considered her voice too 'poppy', so used a soul sample instead) was a blast of upbeat, commercial drum'n'bass, the sirens in the mix this time reminding you that summer in the city, notwithstanding the traffic, air pollution and grime, doesn't have to spell trouble – it can signal party time. The word "celebrate" resonated as Dizzee was pictured gazing lasciviously at the skimply dressed, fake-tanned girls in town, his lecherous leering undercut by wry observations and declaration that life can be improved by a little luck and hard graft – if there was a leitmotiv on *Maths + English*, it was the exhilaration that comes with escape, with tearing up the plans and starting again.

'Bubbles' was slower but fizzed with invention, the burbling keyboard sounds decorating a track that was a dual celebration of Dizzee's beloved Nike Air trainers and the trappings of success. Life, he described, is a jungle, but there was no question here, as there seemed to be on *Showtime*, that he was going to sink. By contrast, 'Excuse Me Please' was slow, laid-back but mellifluously jazzy in its intricacy, with another nice, neat configuration of keyboard notes. The track might have made a suitable album closer at an earlier stage in his career: it found Dizzee poised to give it all up, baffled, bothered and bewildered by the madness, evil and confusion surrounding him. It was a standard-issue "conscious" rap song about the iniquities of the world in which the rich prospered and the poor foundered, with the protagonist wandering the godless terrain, wondering who was in charge of it all before deciding he wanted to take physical issue with the big boss, i.e. God.

'Hardback (Industry)' contrasted starkly with the previous song's dazed and confused air, being a series of info-bites on how to survive in a hard, unforgiving world. Harsh, but shot through with a sense of play and nervous energy, it wasn't quite as startlingly original as anything on *Boy In Da Corner*, but with its eerie Bernard Herrmann-ish strings and John Carpenter-esque menacing synth burble it added to the impression of an artist once more on top of his game. The advice offered by Dizzee on 'Hardback (Industry)' was succinct and simple: in this life, especially the corner of the universe known as the music industry, you need to keep your wits about you (back straight, face stern) to survive. Directing his attention at wannabes, he advised them to be original; with Nick Cage in mind, he counselled them to find a decent manager; when you're casting around for a record contract, he warned hopefuls to be alert for when the record label makes empty promises and to make sure they find a one that isn't peopled by blowheads, one that lets you be creatively free but guarantees you maximise your commercial potential. If and when the hits come and stardom beckons, you need to change your number because ghouls and groupies will start calling; be careful what you say to journalists because bad news travels fast these days; don't spend all your money because the taxman will want his share. Then Dizzee got all sober and serious: buy a house, he recommended, preferably not on a council estate – your Porsche won't last long there. Finally, he suggested, enjoy what you do because nothing lasts forever. Wise words, climaxing what was possibly the most sensible, practical cut-out-and-keep guide in the hip hop canon, US or UK; he could have sold it separately on the internet as a pamphlet.

There followed two tracks with unexpected guest appearances. 'Temptation' featured the vocals and guitar of Alex Turner, frontman with Sheffield indie band Arctic Monkeys; it was a version of a song called 'Temptation Greets You Like Your Naughty Friend', originally the B-side of the Monkeys' single 'Brianstorm'. The track didn't do Dizzee's crossover ambitions any harm, even if it didn't quite signal the start of a new grime/indie hybrid, only semi-jokingly heralded by the *NME* at the time as "grindie". Another ode to the power of positive thinking, over a fast, skittering rhythm, 'Temptation' heard Dizzee this time offering himself advice, telling himself to keep strong, not to believe his own hype, to keep it real, to stay out of the limelight, avoid temptation and accept that there's more to life than narcotics and celebrity. The second guest-star vehicle, 'Wanna Be', was a collaboration with Lily Allen – some thought the genial ribbing in the song about having his "bling" bought by his mum was a bit rich coming from a former pupil of public school Bedales, but once again the presence of such a big mainstream star demonstrated Dizzee's appeal across the board and his status as the Brit hopper it was cool to collaborate with. It worked both ways: it seemed as though everyone was queuing up for some Dizzee cachet. With a sample of 'So You Wanna Be A Boxer' from the 1976 movie musical *Bugsy Malone* and Allen's typically squeaky-voiced chorus/refrain, 'Wanna Be' was like a jolly playground chant or a nursery rhyme, or a grime-age *Mary Poppins* number, and although it was far better

Backstage at Glastonbury in 2009. (NAKI/REDFERNS)

Dizzee and Calvin Harris performing onstage for BBC Radio 1 at Glastonbury in 2009. (NAKI/REDFERNS)

Glastonbury, 2009. (PHOTO BY NAKI/REDFERNS)

Supporting The Prodigy at Wembley Arena in April 2009. (ANDY SHEPPARD/REDFERNS)

Dizzee with his Best Dancefloor Filler award at the *NME* Awards in 2009. (DAVE HOGAN/GETTY IMAGES)

"He gets better with age": leaving the *GQ* Men Of The Year Awards at The Royal Opera House, September 2009.
(PHOTO BY DANNY MARTINDALE/FILMMAGIC)

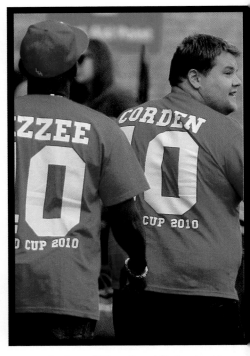

James Corden and Dizzee Rascal filming the video to 2010's World Cup Anthem, 'Shout For England'.
(BERETTA/SIMS/REX FEATURES)

They got the love: Florence Welch with Dizzee Rascal performing at the Brit Awards, London, February 16, 2010.
(PICTURE BY JOHN MARSHALL/LFI)

Giddy up, horsey: backstage in Queensland with Lily Allen in January 2010. (LYNDON MECHIELSEN/NEWSPIX/REX FEATURES)

Onstage at the O2 Arena, March 7, 2010. (NEIL LUPIN/REDFERNS)

than 'Dream' from *Showtime* (which also had a cheerful sampled chorus that made it palatable to minors) it actually harked back to the novelty UK reggae-rap of Smiley Culture's mid-Eighties smash 'Cockney Translation'. Lily and Dizzee traded verses and insults (the unpleasant word "spastic" gets an airing) but the overall tone was good-natured, rhyming "wally" with "Corrie", while Dizzee once again showed he was turning his back on his petty-criminal past, confirming his new, positive outlook.

The closing track of the UK version of *Maths + English*, 'U Can't Tell Me Nuffin'', ended the album on a quietly triumphant note. Setting what sounded like the staccato, stabbing strings from Bernard Herrmann's soundtrack to *Psycho* to avant-grime beats, it caught Dizzee in belligerent mood, owning up to youthful indiscretions (with a reference to his madnesses), recalling his dramatic scrapes in, for example, Ayia Napa, and renouncing everything that stood in the way of mainstream acceptance. The reference to bouncing to the music provided as neat a nod towards his next transition – to fully fledged dance-pop sensation with 'Dance Wiv Me' – as you could wish for, as he flipped the bird to doubters, who he declaimed in uncomplimentary terms.

Maths + English went gold in the UK, selling over 100,000 copies. It entered the chart at number seven, one position higher than *Showtime* and considerably higher than the number 23 managed by *Boy In Da Corner*. There were far greater highs to come, but the measured success of *Maths + English* did prove that Dizzee Rascal was no one-album wonder. It was also testament to his new positive approach, one that would soon pay tremendous dividends.

CHAPTER 14

Seems 2 Be

"I'm not glorifying bad situations, I'm trying to make them into art. Every album I do is hopefully a living, breathing thing. There is always going to be negative shit in there, because I'm a person and I'm no saint."

Dizzee Rascal

Maths + English was, in the main part, generously received by the press, who seemed delighted that Dizzee Rascal was back on course after the temporary slump that was *Showtime*. The BBC review congratulated him on producing "a hip hop record with the world in its sights" and praised his decision to distance himself from a grime scene that had thus far failed to deliver in commercial terms. It described 'Pussyole (Old Skool)' as "the most accessible song he's ever recorded", acknowledging that the album as a whole found Dizzee "in party mode" with "introspection in moderation". 'Flex' and 'Wanna Be' were both "sure-fire hits", while, it asserted, "Dizzee's ear for a pop hook is more acute than ever". Apart from album closer, 'You Can't Tell Me Nuffin', the BBC review concluded that "this is a bid for the big time. [And] if that means leaving behind the insular scene that bore him, then so be it."

Most critics took one look at the sleeve credits, zeroing in on the names Lily Allen and Alex Turner, and concluded, rightly, that this was Dizzee's lunge for mainstream acceptance, give or take the occasional allusions to gang violence. *The Guardian* reviewer agreed that Dizzee was right to explore broader horizons than a grime scene that had seemingly gone back underground. To writer Alex Macpherson, *Maths + English* was a classic summer album – only this was summer not as "endurance test", but "a season for endless parties, dancing in the streets and kissing random strangers". He concluded that Dizzee "the twitchy, nervy kid" was no more, replaced by a pragmatist with commercial nous: "This is Dizzee Rascal's pop album: catchy and danceable."

In a mixed review, the *NME* stated that, "With grime less ascendant in the mainstream than it once threatened to be, Dizzee finds himself head of a decapitated scene." This, it decided, was his "straightest record yet", one that delved into "crunk, rock, drum'n'bass and pop with varying results". It praised 'Where's Da G's' – "a slick Americanised electro banger, taking G-funk from its sloping LA roots and hotwiring it through the engine of a Baby Bentley" – and 'Temptation' ("[it] brilliantly twists Alex Turner's voice through subtle dub reverb, totally justifying the band's appearance"). But it was negative about 'Suk My Dick' ("mindlessly idiotic"), 'Da Feelin' ("unforgivably naff nonsense") and 'Hardback (Industry)' ("a bit dull"). Following the previous month's cover story, the *Observer Music Monthly* review was short and sweet. "Without labouring the point, can we just reiterate that young Dylan Mills' third outing is his strongest, most ambitious and mature record to date. It's wider reaching in its lyrical content and, more importantly, in its musical range. Essential."

As ever, the American press explored Dizzee's latest opus more deeply than their Brit counterparts. In its three-and-a-half-star review, rock bible *Rolling Stone* wrote: "*Maths + English* is long on dark, dense, electro beats and frazzled techno, plus frantic-but-ballsy rhymes that even Brits might have trouble parsing." In its typically long and thoughtful review, music website Pitchfork wondered whether the image of Dizzee on the back cover of the album, with his middle finger raised in a defiant US-style "fuck-you", would affect distribution, and therefore sales, of the record in the States following the poor performance of its predecessor. "It says a lot about [label] XL's lack of faith in the US market for grime's international ambassador," wrote Nate Patrin, who nevertheless saw signs of an increased musical Americanisation on Dizzee's part throughout *Maths + English*. Lyrically, meanwhile, Patrin admired Dizzee's ability to take "even the more well-worn hip hop subjects – paranoia, phonies, how to survive the music industry – [and make them] flow viciously in a manner that's just about as good as anybody alive when it comes to completing the sound of a production".

All Music concurred with the assertion that Dizzee's music had an increasingly American feel, suggesting that it was "more rooted in Southern bounce than anything else" and comparing the track 'Sirens', with its "tense narrative over a chaotic production that throws neck-snapping percussion, head-banging guitars, and sound effects into a whirlwind of manic energy", to "early, agitated Cypress Hill". It did, however, consider *Maths + English* overall to be Dizzee "at his least unique and least riveting, both sonically and lyrically, thus far". *Entertainment* magazine determined that the "Brit prince of bravado", despite occasional signs of "vim and vigour", had gone soft with all the mainstream cameos, but assumed that it was a pragmatic move: "Consider this Rascal's bid for Stateside stardom – he's no longer that *Boy in Da Corner*." In an eight out of ten review, Pop Matters was delighted that, despite setting himself "an awfully high bar" with his previous two albums, here "Rascal manages to outdo himself, releasing one of the most memorable and challenging hip hop albums in recent memory." Reviewer Matthew Fiander liked the way Dizzee's emotions "were all over the map": confessional on 'World Outside', self-destructive on 'Paranoid', and so on. "In a genre increasingly driven by persona, Dizzee Rascal is a gritty but earnest breath of fresh air," wrote Fiander. "This is an album packed with a number of equations: Dizzee Rascal as grimy rapper, as music star, as angry young man, as concerned and hopeful world citizen."

Lastly, *Stylus* magazine struck the sourest note. It diagnosed Dizzee with suffering from "the sophomore slump" – more usually known in the UK as "second album syndrome", even though, of course, this was his third. Writer Ian Cohen found Dizzee suffering from a bad case of the "what now?"s following his début and *Showtime*, wondering what to do for an encore. "The first two words that come to mind when evaluating *Maths + English*," he declaimed, "are 'flossy' and 'inconsistent'." Cohen judged *Maths + English* to be a failed attempt on the part of the grime scene's prime mover to produce "a globetrotting party record". OK were the upbeat jams on which Dizzee could be found "playing the role of playboy jetsetter and loving every minute of it" (Cohen described 'Da Feelin'' as a "bonkers drum'n'bass/Kanye hybrid", as though he knew what was coming next). But the set was almost too diverse, lacking cohesion, in places even "embarrassingly juvenile" ('Suk My Dick'), while 'Wanna Be' made Cohen especially gloomy: "I doubt 2007 will bring a worse offense to my ears than 'Wanna Be'," he wrote. "You'll need the tolerance of Jack Bauer to get through the first 20 seconds without wishing great pain on Lily Allen." And 'You Can't Tell Me Nuffin'' wasn't much better, "[closing] the record on an atypically churlish and defensive note". In summing up, *Stylus* considered *Maths + English* to be a record less likely to be remembered for its successes than for its failures.

If some US critics were sniffy about *Maths + English*, the feeling in the UK was that Dizzee had arrested the decline begun by *Showtime*. In July 2007, 'Pussyole (Old Skool)' became the second single to be released from the album. His eighth single overall, it reached number 22 in the main chart and topped the indie singles chart for a week, its appearance on radio programmers' playlists eased presumably by the contraction of the title to the rather less offensive 'Old Skool' ("pussyole" being a slang term of abuse – for a generally untrustworthy person, a fake friend – which Dizzee himself is widely regarded as having popularised). For the "clean version" of the single, the chorus was removed due to the preponderance of "pussyole"s, although the "explicit version" was also on there for those with less delicate sensibilities. There was also a track on the CD single called 'My Life', which featured Newham Generals.

A third single, 'Flex', was lifted off *Maths + English* in November 2007. This time there was no brand new material, just variations (remixes, dub versions) on the lead track. It charted one place below its predecessor in the main chart, but spent twice as long at the top of the indie chart. The video was an entertaining affair. It showed Dizzee dozing off in front of the TV, unable to find anything interesting to watch, and dreaming of an *X Factor*-style talent show called 'The Flex Factor', complete with inimitable Dirtee Stank logo. It starred Dizzee as one of three judges on the show, in a black wig that didn't make him look any more like Simon Cowell than he did bald, along with actor/TV presenter/DJ Reggie Yates and an attractive unknown woman who feigned boredom with the contestants throughout. Fellow rap laureate Mike Skinner, aka The Streets, also made a cameo in the video as one of the performers, apparently reading a book of verse (to which Dizzee the judge responded by reading a newspaper), as did Peterborough United footballer Gabriel Zakuani and magician Dynamo. Instead of singing, each of the contestants on 'The Flex Factor' danced, but none of them impressed the judges apart from two black-clad females, who unsurprisingly won.

In a lengthy report, Ben Thompson of *Observer Music Monthly* noted that with "Kiss FM-worthy dance tracks" such as 'Flex' – and he was perhaps also thinking of its accompanying video – Dizzee was displaying a new, light attitude. "It feels," he wrote, "as if a weight has been lifted from his shoulders." Dizzee concurred when he replied, cheerfully: "A lot of raves, a lot of drugs, and a lot of sex have kind of accounted for some of that." He agreed that his hedonistic phase had helped calm him down, adding that more than anything it was the new upbeat response of his audience that had brought his change of outlook. "It's a different kind of energy [now]," he said. "There's no feeling like seeing however many thousand people jumping up and down, bubbling and happy, all because of you. I could do that all day and all night. The world would be a better place if it was just about that."

One thing that *Maths + English* didn't win was the 2007 Mercury Music Prize, although it was nominated alongside the previous year's winners, Arctic Monkeys, as well as Amy Winehouse, Bat For Lashes, Jamie T and several more. Dizzee was given odds of 33/1 at the bookies, and most expected Winehouse to win for her worldwide smash *Back To Black*, but it was 'nu rave' indie band The Klaxons who emerged victorious with their album *Myths Of The Near Future*.

Despite this being the period that saw Dizzee Rascal moving ever closer to the bright pop light, there were still dark times. In 2008, it was reported that 'Dean', the extra track on his 'Sirens' CD single, was being released separately in aid of suicide charity C.A.L.M. (all proceeds from the single were to go to the Campaign Against Living Miserably) and to raise awareness of the problem of suicide among 15 to 35-year-old men; the song was about a friend of Dizzee's, Dean Munroe, who took his own life in 2003.

The single could be downloaded as a music video from iTunes, and was, said the rapper of his late friend, about "not being closer to him, not seeing it". Over a slow beat and sorrowful melody, the lyrics, recounting Dizzee's memories of Munroe, were poignant in the extreme, especially when they detailed the build-up to his death, with allusions to be the soul-rupturing pain he must have endured, and there was even mention of his method of self-cancellation (jumping off the balcony of a high-rise flat). The song also offered a glimpse of the meditative man behind the increasingly jolly public face, positing the idea that, although you could take the boy out of Bow, you couldn't take Bow out of the boy. A mournful, reflective lyric posited the idea that, for Dizzee, success and stardom helped keep his own negative thoughts at bay.

He went on to explain to *Newsbeat* that he and Munroe had been friends since school and had lived near each other in Bow. "He was one of the first people I'd ever known to have died and how he died was a bit of a shock," he confessed. "I didn't quite know how to feel." As soon as he got news of his friend's death, he wrote the rap for him, around the time he was working on *Maths + English*. And although it didn't make the cut, C.A.L.M. picked up on it and he made a video for it. Dizzee added that, for him, charity work was essential, especially for an issue that had such personal connotations. "If it's a way I can give back, then it's my duty," he said. C.A.L.M. director Jane Powell explained that all profits from the single would go towards running the charity's hotline, and that raising awareness about the matter was crucial (three young men commit suicide every day).

"The key for us is putting out the message that strong isn't silent and having someone like Dizzee get this message out is just fantastic," she said. "Young men listen, for the most part, to other young men, rather than charities or government spokespeople." Furthered Dizzee: "Everyone's talking about gun crime and knife crime and a lot of people are suffering because of it, but people are doing more harm to themselves, killing themselves. With things like C.A.L.M., you can talk to them cos that is the main thing – talking."

In July 2008, Dizzee suffered another tragic loss when a former girlfriend, 23-year-old Kaya Bousquet, a dancer who had appeared in music videos for R Kelly, Westlife and The Streets, died in a car crash along with three of her friends. She had been involved in a high-speed collision when a lorry ploughed into her hatchback, which had run out of petrol on the M1 motorway. She had been his live-in girlfriend for two years apparently, and according to her sister Sequoia, he was terribly upset: "Dizzee was devastated by her death and has been to her grave with me since," she told reporters.

There was more distress for Dizzee when he was arrested by a police dog handler following an alleged incident on Friday

December 12, 2008, in Sevenoaks Way, Orpington, Kent, involving a baseball bat – he was accused of chasing after a driver with the bat after a road-rage row. He was held on suspicion, at Bromley police station, of possessing an offensive weapon, before being released on bail to return to the station later the same month. He ended up with a caution.

Mere days after the incident, his protégés Newham Generals put a song on the net called 'Violence', which featured a rap from Dizzee that seemed to make his position clear on the subject of self-arming and self-protection when it came to violent altercations on the streets. In the lyrics he claims to not be resistant to violence and that, despite wanting to be a good Christian, he's got too much rage in his system. Ultimately, Dizzee was unrepentant and unapologetic, even going so far as to reference the weapons he'd be prepared to use in a confrontational situation: The coda was belligerent to say the least.

Later, Dizzee tempered these words by suggesting he was using a particularly vivid form of poetic licence. "I'm not glorifying [these situations], I'm trying to make them into art," he said. "Everyone likes a little urban story." He added: "Every album I do is hopefully a living, breathing thing – I want it to be real and I want it to be jumping out and affecting people. There is always going to be mad shit and negative shit in there, because I'm a person and I'm no saint, and those things are a part of me." But he also acknowledged his new-found responsibilities as a role model with a large audience of young, impressionable fans. "I want to give something back, especially knowing that there's youngsters listening."

It was this new awareness, this new conscientiousness, even, that was helping to shape his future direction. *Maths + English* had, Dizzee revealed, started life as another dour meditation on the parlous state of the world, "because that was kind of where my head was at the time". It was only by immersing himself in more upbeat music – "old OutKast stuff, Young Jeezy, Dem Franchize Boyz, D4L's 'Laffy Taffy': that whole Atlanta 'snap' thing" – combined with the sheer power of positive thinking, that made

Maths + English the mostly exuberant affair that it became. "It got me back into the mould of that jump-up party shit," he said. And that seemed to be the only way forward for Dizzee, for now. "I wanted to make banging tunes," he said later, "tunes that people can bump to and be ignorant to."

CHAPTER 15

Everybody Dance

"Mr Rascal has managed to appeal to retro-loving disco freaks, clubbers, grimers and mum and dad in one fell swoop."
Respondent to Radio 1 music blog

In June 2008, Dizzee Rascal released a single that would signal his emergence as a true crossover artist and start the process by which he would become the biggest pop star in Britain. 'Dance Wiv Me' was a grime/dance/R&B hybrid that saw Dizzee collaborate with Scottish DJ, producer and singer-songwriter Calvin Harris, as well as R&B vocalist Chrome. The track was co-written by Dizzee and Harris, who apparently recorded their parts separately and then sent them back and forth via computer or the phone, although Chrome was actually in the studio with Dizzee when he laid down his vocals. Dizzee explained to BBC Radio 1 presenter Jo Whiley how their collaboration came about: the rapper had been enormously impressed by Harris' retro electro-pop Top 10 hit 'Acceptable In The 80s' released the previous year, after which the pair met at Radio 1's Big Weekend music event in Preston. It was there that Dizzee admitted to Harris that his single had reignited his passion for music. Would Harris be interested in making a record with him?

"Dizzee texted me, saying he'd done this a cappella over someone else's music, but his verse was too good for their music, so could he do it with me instead?" recalled Harris in the press release that accompanied his 2009 album, *Ready For The Weekend* (which included the extended mix of the single). "So I spent a long time on it, to make sure it lived up to his expectations. I sent him the track, and he called me at two in the morning to say it was amazing, so I knew it was good."

Harris' contribution duly completed, he sent the track to Dizzee's studio for him to work on. The latter proceeded to pen some lyrics for himself to rap and Chrome and Harris to sing – a lightweight affair about teasing another man's girlfriend away from him and onto the dance floor in a nightclub. Amazingly, the Londoner and the Scot never met again after the Big Weekend in Preston, such were the wonders of modern technology. Explained Dizzee in an interview with BBC's *Newsbeat*: "Me and Calvin met and we exchanged numbers [but] we never actually met once to actually make the tune; we did it back and forth over the phone. It was good, we were just like, 'What about changing that hook a bit?' Chrome was the only one that came in the studio but it was good working with him because we've done a few things in the past."

An irresistible, infectious number just made for the summer season, 'Dance Wiv Me', Dizzee's 10th single, was released digitally on June 30, 2008 (it was made available in the shops in physical format one week later). It spent four weeks at pole position in the UK – his first Top 10 hit since 'Stand Up Tall' in 2004 – and eventually became the 12th biggest-selling single of the year, as well as the 79th best-seller of the decade; it also earned a platinum disc for sales of 600,000. It fared well in the Irish charts, too, reaching number five, while in Australia it peaked at number 13, where it was certified gold, with sales in excess of 35,000. Sales were presumably helped by the numerous live versions and remixes of the song on offer by such producers and DJs as Jason Nevins and Dirty Vegas (it was also noted by the Song Facts website that this was "the first deliberately misspelt UK chart-topper since the Pussycat Dolls' number one hit 'Stickwitu' in December 2005" – perhaps such cheeky licence with the English language helped it gain traction with the public). Dizzee, Harris and Chrome performed an impromptu acoustic rendition of the song for the BBC as part of its 2008 coverage of the Glastonbury festival; it was this version that later featured in an episode of HBO's highly rated US comedy-drama *Entourage*.

'Dance Wiv Me' was a transitional release for Dizzee for two reasons. First, it was his début release on his own Dirtee Stank label after breaking away from XL over debates about his musical direction; and it was his first no-holds-barred commercial dance-pop release (ironically, it reached number one just one month after Wiley's only marginally less radio-friendly 'Wearing My Rolex' reached number two). It is alleged that, after playing the song to the boss of his former record company, the latter wasn't convinced that this sort of commercial R&B-pop was the way forward for the rapper, and so Dizzee decided to release it himself. Recalling his conversation with XL, he told *The Daily Telegraph* in 2009: "I said, 'OK, you like to be thought of as edgy, I get that, but now the person who gave you the edgiest album you've ever put out [i.e. *Boy In Da Corner*] is offering you a straight-up pop track. You haven't forced me to do this, I found my way there myself: you should be pleased.'" He added: "It was a blessing, though, because I got to do it myself."

Dizzee was right: he had single-handedly pushed music forward with *Boy In Da Corner* and taken the experimental post-garage sound as far as it could go; now it was time to move towards the mainstream, a shift in direction that he had thoroughly earned the right to make. As he explained to *The Daily Star*, it was all very well being a cult hero on the margins, but there was no good reason why British rappers shouldn't reap the benefits of success with a more streamlined dance-pop sound, and never mind the accusations of "selling out". Besides, for Dizzee, 'Dance Wiv Me' was no less experimental than anything he had done before; it was just a different kind of experiment. "Experimenting with dance music is a good way for British rappers to get on the radio and into the charts," he reasoned. "Some people might see this as me selling out, but no way. Every track I write I try to make different from the last and as my profile has risen with all the festivals and live shows I've done, I've wanted to experiment more."

In a blog for the BBC Radio 1 website in 2010, on the back of Dizzee's number one smash with 'Dirtee Disco', opinion-former Fraser McAlpine summed up the attitude of the pro-chartbound Dizzee brigade when he wrote: "Man, I love Dizzee Rascal. I mean I REALLY love Dizzee Rascal. You'd have to be the killjoy of all time – or, yes, someone with a legitimate grudge – to feel any differently, surely? He's a talented, articulate pop star with something to say and the means to deliver it, so that's all great for starters. But he's also incredibly good at winding up hipsters. And as we all know, winding up hipsters is, if not our sole reason to be allowed to draw air into our lungs, probably the most important thing we will ever do." He continued in sarcastic vein: "Fancy a proper street-level UK hip hop artist with tons of credibility and a Mercury Award reducing his once-mighty muse to the level of silly pop songs? How vulgar! Fancy a street-level UK hip hop artist dallying with DISCO, of all things. How common! Fancy a street-level UK hip hop artist selling out by writing songs about enjoying yourself, on a dancefloor..." Respondents to the blog were in accord. As one wrote: "Mr Rascal has managed to appeal to retro-loving disco freaks, clubbers, grimers and mum and dad in one fell swoop." Besides, as a commentator on *The Guardian* website pointed out, Dizzee had had to deal with accusations of "selling out" as soon as his video for 'I Luv U' had appeared on MTV Base five years earlier.

Most observers seemed to approach 'Dance Wiv Me' with caution, assuming it to be the trashiest "chav" disco confection imaginable, only to be won over by its easy-going charms. As music site Digital Spy wrote: "A collaboration between irritating, Eighties-obsessed singer Calvin Harris and UK grime merchant Dizzee Rascal sounds on paper like a pretty horrendous proposition. When news leaked that the pair had created a 'party banger', most people's heads sank further. But 'Dance Wiv Me' isn't a disaster – shockingly, it's actually rather good."

The video was directed by Mark Anthony and featured Dizzee and Chrome seated in a club joined by cocktail-sipping, bling-draped party people, with the former pair predictably surrounded by girls in perilously tiny denim hotpants. Chorus-singer Calvin Harris was cast in the role of DJ and barman. At the end of the video, Dizzee and Chrome leave the club with some ladies, but what was most striking about it was Dizzee's performance and ease in front of the camera – he seemed as at home in this conventionally glamorous locale as he had in those gritty *verité* promos for his early grime singles, exuding a natural charm, winking and smiling and wiggling his hips.

Not that he'd undergone a complete personality transformation; he hadn't totally lost touch with his thoughtful, introspective side. In an interview with Ed Marriot of *The Times* in summer 2008 entitled 'Rebel With A Cause', Dizzee talked openly about the value of religion in his life, the role of late martial artist Bruce Lee in his spiritual development ("He's a philosopher, a deep guy. I've been reading his autobiography, *Artist Of Life*, and there's a lot of insight into the soul, the world, life in general"), the counselling he had as a child, his relationship with his mother, and the death of his friend Dean Munroe – the article ended with a plug for the C.A.L.M. helpline (see Chapter 14) and website address.

Speaking about his faith, Dizzee said: "I was raised in the Church and, yeah, I pray sometimes. But I talk to God in my own way, and my own time." He revealed that, beyond recording and performing, he liked to travel to hot countries, jet-ski and "drink nice alcohol with a nice pretty girl", while also admitting that old habits die hard: "But I might go and sit with my friends in a council estate and smoke weed, too," he said. "I smoke a bit of weed for stress. But I'm not the kind of person who overdoes it. I don't go on three-day drug binges. I don't fall out of clubs drunk". (In fact, he reiterated this point two years later to *The Independent* when he said: "I'm not having any alcohol. No weed. I'm not doing anything – except some boxing to release energy. I'm tired of partying, it's boring, the same people, the same chat. I like staying in. I'm that kind of guy.") Finally, and most poignantly, he confessed to still feeling anguish at the suicide of his schoolfriend Dean. "It must have been super-rough for him to have killed himself," he said. "I still don't know quite what drove him to it. We have all been there, felt really low, back against the wall, as if the world is definitely against us." In summing up, in the light of all these views and beliefs, journalist Marriot wrote: "It feels increasingly unfair to tar him with this tired bad-boy cliché. Here, for all his macho front, is a young man struggling, in his words, to be 'real'."

Perhaps the best example of the new, frivolous, fun-size Dizzee combining with the edgy, marginal, serious Dizzee came when he appeared, on November 5, 2008, on BBC2's *Newsnight*. He was invited to appear on the programme for a discussion with hard-hitting presenter Jeremy Paxman and Baroness Amos, the former International Development Secretary, about the likelihood of Barack Obama's success in becoming President of the United States being repeated in the UK. What, wondered Paxman, did Dizzee make of it? "It's positive," he replied, talking to the presenter on a TV monitor, from a studio elsewhere in London. "It's positive because he [Obama] is mixed race as well, so he is an immediate symbol of unity." He added that he believed hip hop music played a crucial part in bringing Obama to the White House. "I don't think he could have won it without hip hop. Hip hop is what encouraged the youth to, um, get involved in voting and making the place better and he is the first president to embrace it." Did he, furthered Paxman, see his success being achieved by a black Briton? Dizzee believed so. "In time. Yeah, man." Paxman was taken aback. "You're rather positive!" he exclaimed, to which the rapper replied: "Why not, man? There's a first time for everything, isn't there? Everything takes time. If you believe you can achieve, innit?" Moving the debate on, Paxman then asked Dizzee whether he believed in political parties in Britain. "Yeah, they exist," he answered. "I believe in 'em ... I don't know if I care. I don't know if it makes a difference. But you know what I mean. It is what it is. Politicians are gonna say what they say – you might get every now and again a genuine one, innit? But I think people, like, as a whole make the difference. I don't think one party can make a difference." Typically combative, Paxman tried to pick holes in Dizzee's rhetoric, saying, "But in the end you've already told us how excited you feel about the election of a black president, [so] clearly an individual does make a difference?" Dizzee wasn't fazed. "Yeah, to help boost the morale," he smiled. "But change comes from everybody coming together and making a difference." Baroness Amos then talked about the changing nature of Britishness, which prompted Paxman to ask Dizzee whether he considered himself British. He was good-naturedly shocked by the question. "Of course I'm British, man! You know me! I'm here, man – what's good. I think it don't matter what colour you are, it matters what colour your heart is and your intentions. I think a black man, purple man, Martian man can run the country, as long as he does right by the people." Paxman then put Dizzee on the spot. "Well," he ventured, "why don't you run for office?" This time, there was a big, broad grin. "See, that's a very good idea. I might have to do that one day. Dizzee Rascal for prime minister, yeah! Wassappenin'!" Finally, Dizzee once again praised hip hop's role in the inauguration of America's first black president. "Barack Obama embraced hip hop, man. That's the way he got through to kids. There was a more young vote than ever. And it was through hip hop!"

Not everyone was happy with the Paxman/Rascal face-off. Some believed Dizzee came out of the interview looking inarticulate, unintelligent and ill-informed, blaming Paxman in the process. British soul singer Estelle (best known for her 2008 number one duet with Kanye West, 'American Boy'), to name just one, accused the BBC presenter of treating Dizzee, at best, patronisingly, at worst like a fool. She told the *New Statesman*, "I was like, 'He is taking you for an idiot right now! Did no one brief you?' Paxman's not going to get away with asking me, 'Do I think I'm British?'" The BBC responded by saying, "The topics being discussed were race, nationality and identity, and this question was a natural part of that discussion." Another British R&B performer, Craig David, weighed in to the debate. He had mixed feelings about the programme. On the one hand, he thought the rapper was just "Dizzee being Dizzee"; on the other, he did feel that he could have approached the situation with a little more intellectual rigour and worried that the swaggering bravado he displayed (it was actually more childlike glee) played up to people's image of the stereotypical bad-boy grime MC. As for Paxman, he didn't believe he was being racist during the *Newsnight* debate, but he did wonder whether Dizzee was really the right man for the job of being interviewed on a programme on such an auspicious occasion, one with the gravitas of *Newsnight*. The jury, as far as Craig David was concerned, was still out.

Meanwhile, over at *The Guardian* website, journalist Paul Moody decided that Paxman was, given the "paradigm shift in global consciousness" in the wake of Obama's victory, in a grouchy mood even by his standards. "His treatment of Dizzee Rascal on yesterday's *Newsnight* beggared belief," he wrote. "Like a sadistic QC determined to dispatch this young ruffian to new digs in Wandsworth, he seemed eager to prove that the overnight improvement in intergenerational, interracial understanding has no place here." Moody's perception of it was that Paxman was "clearly livid at having Britain's premier MC on the show to add some street-level zing to the debate." He mused: "Was it jet-lag, Barack-ache, or just news that M&S shares have slumped that got our man's knickers in a twist? Or cast-iron proof that, until the political hierarchy stop looking down their noses, any dreams of racial integration on this side of the pond will remain just that?"

But others watching the encounter between Paxman and Rascal concluded that the rapper won on points. As the Excite website wrote: "It's a rare feat to make political interrogator Jeremy Paxman feel uncomfortable during an interview but Dizzee Rascal seems to have managed it. Talking on *Newsnight* last night the legendary hip hopper's urban street jive on the US election puts even poor old Jezza into a bit of a spin. Dizzee for prime minister!"

Such was the speed at which Dizzee Rascal was infiltrating the mainstream and becoming a household name, it suddenly didn't seem strange or outlandish to imagine him at some stage entering politics and using the platform to give voice to a generation. But not just yet. He was still only 23 and there was plenty of fun to be had. First, he needed to go bonkers.

CHAPTER 16

Freaky Freaky

"If you are going to work, you might as well follow your heart, because nothing in life is easy and if it's going to be hard, it might as well be what you really want."

Dizzee Rascal

On May 18, 2009 Dizzee Rascal released the single – again on his own record label, Dirtee Stank – that would become his second number one and make him unquestionably the biggest solo male pop star in Britain. It was his latest high-profile collaboration, following those with Basement Jaxx, Lily Allen, Arctic Monkeys and Calvin Harris; this time it was with American producer, DJ and remixer Armand Van Helden, who was most famous in the UK for his remix of Tori Amos' 'Professional Widow', which reached number one in 1996, and for his own solo number one in 1999 with 'U Don't Know Me'.

The single was called 'Bonkers' and it was, following on from 'Dance Wiv Me', the second release from his forthcoming fourth album, *Tongue N' Cheek*. It was immediately put on the Radio 1 playlist (the A list), while presenter Jo Whiley made it her 'Pet

Sound' and Sara Cox anointed it her 'Weekend Anthem'. You could see its appeal a mile off: the music, written by Van Helden, was the most commercial, anthemic electro/house imaginable, with hooks designed to snag the listener from the off, such as the siren-like keyboard noise, the clattering percussion that felt like multiple claps in the ear, the hissing piston sounds, the manically repeated title word and the weird, wobbly bassline that felt like a drill to the skull and seemed to signal some kind of imminent attack – which was about right, because 'Bonkers' was nothing less than sheer aural assault.

The lyrics were also instantly memorable and in-yer-face (or rather, in-yer-ear), and although they comprised just one eight-line verse and one chorus (also eight lines long), each repeated four times, it was enough to do the trick; in a way, the repetitive aspect of the lyrics made them seem even more brilliantly boneheaded, matching the ingenious, deceptively simple music (deceptive because it actually comprised several sections – brusque opening, standard 4/4 dance rhythm for the verse, clattering chorus, smooth R&B bridge, ravey middle-eight, and so forth – bolted together to make it seem like a botch-up of bad edits so as to further jolt the senses).

The song opened with Dizzee experiencing a series of paradoxical emotions, such as waking up daily, only to find himself still dreaming, and punning on the unreality of it all, with "shallow" and "deep" used to make the point – the words functioning both as illogic enhancers, adding to the sense of disorientation felt by Dizzee in the song, and pure nonsense on the level of an Edward Lear. Only this was Lear via John Lydon, aka Johnny Rotten of The Sex Pistols, as the penultimate line of the verse stated in the boldest, loudest terms: All he cared about, he proclaimed, were sex and violence, and his favourite antidote to tranquility was a booming bassline. The lyric was at once totally meaningless and utterly evocative of the all-powerful exhilaration you can experience on a good day or a good night out. 'Bonkers', like the Pistols' 'Anarchy In The UK' and 'God Save The Queen', had about it an air of menace, only this was a more benign kind of terror (it was like being shocked alert by the funny fat orange man in the notorious 'You Know When You've Been Tango'd' TV adverts); everything about it felt inclusive rather than divisive. All you had to do to join Dizzee's 'Bonkers' barmy army was be open to its all-consuming spirit of affirmation (unexpectedly, Simon Reynolds, always one of the best music writers on the subject of Dizzee Rascal, described it as "bubblegum nihilism"). It wasn't even a hedonists' anthem; it was simply pro feeling fine and free. And, on that point, Dizzee was absolutely right: there was nothing crazy about that.

'Bonkers' was indicative of Dizzee's latest brilliant direction: simultaneously insanely addictive and mentally experimental pop music. He embraced pop in such an unembarrassed fashion you couldn't help but warm to it. In an interview with *The Sun*, he admitted that he wasn't the least bit ashamed of the song's pop hooks, and that he was happy, despite an initial reluctance to make house music, with some of the tune's more propulsive grooves. He also revealed that *Tongue N' Cheek* would contain more pop songs than any of his previous albums, and that he had stopped making the sort of grime music evinced on *Boy In Da Corner*. He had expanded his horizons and was delighted to be making a huge splash in the mainstream.

The video that accompanied 'Bonkers' was a suitably exuberant affair. It opened with Dizzee waking up in bed in a Day-Glo turquoise, luxuriously padded cell that turned out to be attached to the back of a moving lorry. It proceeded to show him variously watering some fake plants, grinning broadly in a shark outfit, and dancing with a bunch of clubbers in black scuba-diving gear daubed in fluorescent green paint on the back of another lorry driving through a cartoon city at night. 'Bonkers' was about right.

Backed by another new track, 'Butterfly', which came with its own bonkers video (a series of fast-cut images, including semi-clad girls, Dizzee in a pink bra and a baby apparently munching on a dog's turd), 'Bonkers' did exceedingly well commercially, earning a gold disc for sales in excess of 400,000 in Britain, even if it failed to translate quite as successfully around the world as it might have done (it got to number one in the official UK singles and dance charts and number three in Ireland, but only went Top 10 in Belgium and Top 20 in Australia); critically, it split reviewers, some grime purists offended by the sacrilegious embrace of pop, while more open-minded souls welcomed Dizzee's new direction.

The music website Unreality Shout decided, probably rightly, that 'Bonkers' was going to be the summer's big hen-night party and lads' drinking anthem, the soundtrack to boisterous wassailing in suburban nightclubs for intoxicated revellers of both sexes. Crucially, Dizzee was now appealing not just to inner-city types but to those on the outskirts as well, and he was reaching as many women as he was men, unlike his earlier grime releases, which had a far bigger following among males. "In fact," admitted the reviewer, "if you see me out for the night, I'll be shrieking along with Sharon and Tracey with my finger in the air. Definitely one of my favourite tracks of 2009 so far." Pitchfork, by contrast, disliked Van Helden's "awkward-choppy beats" and Dizzee's "equally awful-choppy hook". And it concluded that, notwithstanding the "pleasantly abrasive grind" and "synth curlicue", it amounted to little more than an inferior take on Wiley's superb number two hit from 2008, 'Wearing My Rolex'.

In a blog for *The Guardian*, Simon Reynolds confessed that it was hard for "early adopter types" like him not to have mixed feelings about Dizzee's volte-face. "It's lovely to see him riding high – the star he always deserved to be," he said, especially delighted because he far preferred 'Bonkers' to "that putrid team-up with Calvin Harris, 'Dance Wiv Me'". But there was also, he said, "a bittersweet feeling of: 'Why, oh why, did this not happen six years ago" with 'I Luv U'?"

Not that Dizzee was overly concerned with doing the right thing at the right time to please the critics. He was just glad to be where he was, as he told *The Mirror* in summer 2009. Interviewed after a spot of kickboxing, one of his hobbies, he revealed that the secret of his success was "making the best music I can for the biggest audience, while maintaining credibility. Discipline is the key." He added, explaining what it felt like to have such a broad audience,

"I play to families now – mums, dads, kids. It's great to make more people happy."

There were certainly plenty of smiling faces in the crowd when he performed live in Chelmsford at the V Festival in August. The *NME* was there for his show as the sun shone on the 4Music stage. He played a selection of material from his first three albums, plus some tracks from his fourth, then only a month away from release. He opened his set with 'Jus' A Rascal', proceeded to play new song 'Road Rage' and followed that with a cover version of 'Paper Planes' by feted Sri Lankan rapper M.I.A., before treating the crowd to some favourites from his back catalogue, including 'Sirens', 'Fix Up, Look Sharp', 'Pussyole (Old Skool)' and 'Flex'. The final three numbers were all from the latter phase of his career: 'Dance Wiv Me', followed by next single 'Holiday', and finally a climactic 'Bonkers'. Apparently, thousands rushed to the front as soon as Dizzee appeared onstage. After playing 'Sirens' he, his MC sidekick and DJ Semtex, organised a cheering competition before prefacing 'Flex' with a dedication to "the ladies". He had become quite the crowd-pleasing showman. And one of the surest signs of the confidence that the audience now had in his ability to deliver was that arguably the best reaction was reserved for 'Holiday', which wouldn't be in the shops until the following Monday.

'Holiday', released on August 24 (digitally) and August 31 (physical copy), was the third single lifted from *Tongue N' Cheek* – even though the album was still a month away from release. Reuniting the 'Dance Wiv Me' team, it was co-written by Dizzee (lyrics) and Calvin Harris (music), produced by Harris – although the vocals on the track were recorded and produced by Nick Cage – and featured the voice of R&B singer Chrome on the chorus. It was originally written by Harris for British girl group The Saturdays, who bizarrely turned it down; bizarre because it was such an infectious song, not to mention a sure-fire hit. It was easy to imagine the girls singing the chorus. Then again, what really made the single so special was Dizzee's characterful input on the verses as he attempted to coax a young lady to join him on holiday – there was something irresistible about his impish wit as he rhymed "so–so" and "low–low" and made a self-deprecating joke about his linguistic abilities. And whether or not a Saturdays version of the track would have kept the amazing final 45 seconds, where it dramatically transformed from a standard dance rhythm into a euphoric full-on hands–in–the–air trance/rave anthem that was perfect for the end of summer, will never be known.

The video was shot in a villa in Ibiza. It featured Dizzee in a scene that strongly resembled Wham!'s own video for their 1983 hit 'Club Tropicana' (which was also shot in Ibiza), alternately dressed in a Hawaiian shirt and a white wide-boy suit and yellow shirt with wing collars, surrounded by legions of bikini-clad babes; it showed how far he had travelled since *Boy In Da Corner*. The initial intention had been to re-create scenes from *Boogie Nights*, the film about the Seventies porn industry starring Burt Reynolds and Mark Wahlberg as Dirk Diggler. The stars and extras must have looked convincing because at one point during filming a busload of scantily clad German swingers turned up at the villa – apparently notorious for holding wild sex parties – and, spying the TV cameras, filming equipment and all the pneumatic babes, automatically assumed Dizzee was in the middle of a porn shoot. "It was very weird," a local taxi driver told *The Sun*. "The Germans must have seen all those girls arriving and thought their luck was in!"

It was all a long way from Bow. But then, by neat contrast, the extra track on the 'Holiday' CD, 'Live Large N In Charge', was a return to his grime roots, with some of the jagged sonics of his début album, although a few commentators saw evidence of an increasing casual misogyny on Dizzee's part in the lyrics that alluded in no uncertain terms to violent sexual acts. In a *Guardian* blog prompted by the release of the *Tongue N' Cheek* album, Chris Cottingham welcomed his new-found crossover success, even the shift from "spiky electronics and screw-faced raps" to the bouncy pop hooks of his last three singles. But he was less than happy with "the side order of misogyny" that came with this new material. He cited as an example album closer 'Bad Behaviour', and the couplet that rhymed vigorous oral sex with a reference to a climactic line from a *Fast*

Show comedy sketch. Complained Cottingham: "The caustic wit of his early releases has been replaced by low-brow banter from a lads night out in Faliraki." He reflected that Dizzee was "squandering his talents by boasting about his sexual swordsmanship", and pre-empted counter-accusations that it was "just a bit of fun – just look at the album title" by comparing Dizzee to misogynistic Seventies comedians. "That's the same excuse Bernard Manning used," wrote Cottingham. "It doesn't wash and Dizzee knows it; he just doesn't care."

Still, none of this made a difference to the success of 'Holiday', which became his third number one single in a row and sold hundreds of thousands of copies. It seemed as though he had become such a loveable Cockney rogue, for most people he really could do no wrong. Even the Royal Family were getting in on the act. That July, at the 02 Wireless Festival in Hyde Park, London, Dizzee and Prince Harry, the latter on a lads' night out of his own, had a surreal encounter backstage. It was following Dizzee's headline set, and by some accounts it almost went horribly wrong and could have seen the rapper wind up in the Tower. It started off badly – it is alleged that Dizzee threatened to punch the third in line to the throne after he made his entrance "while performing 'boxing moves' and giving 'street handshakes'" and generally being overfamiliar with the rapper and his entourage. Rumour has it that the Prince had even burst into a bit of 'Bonkers' when he came face to face with his pop idol.

This was how the tabloids reported the incident. In the broadsheets, however, the encounter was a little more benign. When the story appeared in *The Daily Telegraph*, for example, the contretemps had been downgraded to "Dizzee had joked to the Prince that he would punch him 'in the face' during the private meeting", while the "boxing moves" had been pulled ironically by the Prince on singer Chrome and another rapper, Smurfie Syco (a Dirtee Stank artist), much to everyone's amusement. "We just had a bit of banter and that," said Dizzee. "It was mad. He was... a bit like me, really." During the encounter, Prince Harry apparently demonstrated to Dizzee his rapping skills, and revealed that not just he but also his brother William was a huge fan of his music. Dizzee was unusually lost for words, and they even swapped telephone numbers and agreed to meet up again.

Reflecting on the rapper-meets-royal encounter in the *Telegraph*, Dizzee admitted: "I never saw that one coming. Prince Harry came in and was joking around and being a bit cheeky, so I told him, 'If you weren't royalty I'd have punched you in the face by now'." He added that the royal pin-up "seemed to like that", reasoning: "He's a naughty boy, so he fits in." In fact, Dizzee considered the Prince to be more of a hellraiser than him. "[Prince Harry] and his mates are probably a bit wilder than us," he said. He also decided he needed to work on his "street handshake", but definitely rated him the friendliest famous person he had met so far. "It has to be Prince Harry," said Dizzee afterwards. "Tom Hanks is a real down-to-earth guy and we chatted about Snoop Dogg, because his son is a fan. But Prince Harry – that is proper royalty, man!"

Dizzee had become one of those rare artists with truly wide-ranging appeal, with fans from hardcore grime kids to the sort of people who buy the occasional pop CD in the supermarket, to members of the House of Windsor.

"Fuck it, man, whatever. It's lovely," said Dizzee at the time. "It's nice to know that I can make music for all sorts of people. That was kind of my goal." He also confessed in an interview with *The Guardian* that the most important lesson that life had taught him thus far was that, "If you are going to work, you might as well follow your heart, because nothing in life is easy and if it's going to be hard, it might as well be what you really want." It was a life lesson that surely came in handy during the making of his fourth album, *Tongue N' Cheek*, and perhaps helped him deal with some of the reactions to his latest music.

CHAPTER 17

Doin' It Big

"The way I see it, everyone's looking for a bit of enlightenment, the more outlandish the better. But I want to keep it real with everyone, not just the guys on the estate."

Dizzee Rascal

Dizzee Rascal explained that he got the idea for his fourth album, *Tongue N' Cheek*, at home. But by home he didn't mean the flat that he grew up in with his mother in Bow, east London; no, he meant his new place, a rather larger residence in leafy, suburban Kent. "It's quiet, it's cool," he said in 2009, explaining that the area to which he had recently moved was "still just about a London borough, I think". He told Ben Thompson of *The Daily Telegraph* that he now lived in a country house in the Home Counties with a "big pond, big fish, big whatever". It was the kind of place where, when he moved in, he was able to hold "a little pool party". He couldn't do that where he used to live: "Where I lived before I didn't really invite anyone round," he said, adding that this was exactly how and why the fourth album came to be. "But this time there were about 20 people there, and I suddenly realised that what I needed to do was make an album you could play all the way through without spoiling the party." He elaborated in *Clash* magazine: "I was having a little party at my house. Snoop Dogg's *Doggystyle* album had been on about five times, over and over. I was like, 'Fucking hell, I need to make an album like this. An album you can put on and actually have a party.' I wanted to make music that would make people get up, move and jump about, instead of stand around and want to fucking kill each other. And that's what I've done. *Tongue N' Cheek* is basically a cheeky album, naughty but nice. It's still dealing with some naughty issues but it's on a party vibe fully, all uptempo, upbeat and quite happy."

Dizzee's follow-up to *Maths + English* was released on September 21, 2009. Because it included the number one singles 'Dance Wiv Me', 'Bonkers' and 'Holiday', as well as the song lined up to be the next single, 'Dirtee Disco', plus 'Road Rage', which was mooted by Dizzee, during an interview at the Evolution Festival in Newcastle-upon-Tyne, as a future single, the album felt like a greatest hits collection. It certainly sold like a hits set, going gold within weeks; by February 2010 it had been certified platinum by the British Phonographic Industry – the BPI – for sales of over 300,000, making it the biggest-selling album of his career. In the week of its release, *Tongue N' Cheek* entered the UK album chart at number three, just behind Muse and Madonna, and four places higher than his previous best – number seven with *Maths + English*.

Such was the magnitude of his stardom by this point, the release of the album was announced on a peak-time TV chat show – BBC1's *Friday Night With Jonathan Ross* – during an interview in which Dizzee discussed the music and the direction it was likely to take. He talked in greater detail about which way he was going, musically, in other interviews at the time, where he revealed that he would be swapping grime for pop. Talking to Tim Adams of *The Observer*, he reiterated his desire to "make some party music", having pretty much exhausted the extreme grime route. The latest test was to make bright, commercial pop. "I made hardcore music and that came kind of easy – it was what I knew," he said. "But it was a challenge for me to make a big pop tune."

In *Clash* magazine, he admitted that he had finally got to grips with what was required to be a successful and credible commercial artist. "I get pop music now," he said. "I get what a pop format is, to be up there with the greats and the best." In the early days, he didn't fully understand how to construct a pop tune because the milieu was so different. "I don't think I really knew how to do it when I started out because the environment that I was competing for was the underground pirate radio scene. It was more MC-based. And there ain't been too many things UK-wise and MC-based that have been in the charts. So that was my only reference." It was, he explained, his seven years in the music industry, a full-scale immersion involving festivals and various pop and rock events, that taught him the tricks of the trade. Not that he was entirely unfamiliar with the terrain. "People think the whole pop thing is new to me," he pointed out. "But I toured with Justin Timberlake when I was 19. I did a track with Basement Jaxx around the same time, as well as supporting Red Hot Chili Peppers, Jay-Z, Nas, Sean Paul. I've been exposed to a lot of the biggest things going."

It was his producer and manager, Nick Cage, who had been encouraging him to "go pop", only to do it his way. There was also the feeling that, if he was going to be making music, he might as well make it available to the biggest number of people possible. However, *Tongue N' Cheek*, he promised, would be pop in terms of accessibility, but it wouldn't be a one-genre affair. "I want to get the album out there to show how diverse I really am," he explained. "There are big pop hits, but there's a full-bodied record to show people who are new to me that I've got a lot to offer."

Tongue N' Cheek may have been, broadly speaking, a full-blown foray into pop territory, and yet ironically, as Dizzee pointed out, he would be making his most commercial music to date not on a corporate behemoth but on his own, independent imprint, Dirtee Stank, having parted company with XL the year before. "I had an offer but it weren't the offer I wanted," he said of his former record label. "I did pretty much what I wanted on XL anyway, but it's mad that when it came to me making a progression towards pop music, they didn't get it." He felt particularly justified in going it alone when 'Dance Wiv Me', which XL declined to release, reached number one – the first independent number one single in 14 years. He felt an even greater sense of satisfaction when he repeated the trick with 'Bonkers' and 'Holiday'.

Dizzee's fourth album was not, however, your average cuddly populist fare destined to entertain people of all generations as they crowded round the family stereo. "I know it'll put a smile on people's faces, and I'll smile at the end," said Dizzee. "But as much as everyone loves me at the moment, there are still going to be some outraged parents." The album got off to an explosive start with 'Bonkers', and if that didn't make your elderly relatives' grey hair stand on end, the second track probably would. The lyrics to 'Road Rage' – which in the end was not issued as a single – were written by Dizzee, while the music was provided by Aaron LaCrate and DJ Debonair Samir. LaCrate was a DJ, designer and film producer from East Baltimore who had produced and remixed records for Madonna and Lily Allen, among others, and toured with Mark Ronson, legendary rapper Rakim and Kanye West. His and Samir's music to 'Road Rage' was staccato, jerky and about as far removed from the standard pop song form as you could get, and yet the refrain about not wanting to see road rage, and the bit where Dizzee repeated "beep beep" as a signal to fellow drivers, had the insistent, infectious quality of a pop chant. The song was possibly inspired by the incident of December 2008 when Dizzee was arrested for wielding a baseball bat during a confrontation in south London. The lyrics, with their profanities and aggressive attitude, gave the lie to the idea that Dizzee was now Mr Family Entertainment (and certainly precluded its release as a single).

The same could be said of the track that followed 'Dance Wiv Me' – 'Freaky Freaky', which had words by Dizzee and music by Nick Cage, and saw him compare his hectic love life to that of Public Enemy lothario, Flavor Flav, the rapper with his very own American reality TV show, *Flavor Of Love*. It featured Dizzee's own inimitable approach to safe sex (there is a disdainful recommendation to wear a condom), and references to sex of the oral variety in cinemas and cars. His attitude towards women was almost comically derisory, with a hilarious though juvenile comparison between his sexual appendage and a particular yellow fruit, and an alphabetical roll-call of his conquests from Antoli, Angelina and Alisha to Patrice and Shanice. And yet he made sure during this ironic slow jam to telegraph his moral indignation at the notion of consorting with minors (unless the girl is over 22, he's not playing).

'Can't Tek No More' (words by Dizzee, music by Shy FX) was quite a departure for Dizzee: it was based around a sample from arguably UK reggae's finest moment – 1980's anthemic dub classic 'Warrior Charge' by Aswad – with additional dialogue from the black British youth culture movie *Babylon*, a gritty account of life in Brixton, south London, made the same year. This song also dealt with underage dilemmas, this time the knife crime that stems from poverty, as well as societal ills in general, from the congestion charge to war. "I was at my cousin's and we put that film on," he said, explaining the genesis of the song to *Clash* magazine, alluding to 'Warrior Charge' and *Babylon*. "I fell asleep, but something was rolling in my head and when I woke up they were chanting that actual part that's in the chorus. A few weeks later Shy FX sent me that with a beat. It was a bit of an omen. It's not just about my pressure. It tackles recession, the war that's going on and everyday hardships. That's my first attempt at a reggae track. This whole album's got shit that people wouldn't expect me to do and I'm loving it."

'Chillin'Wiv Da Man Dem' was another excursion into uncharted territory for Dizzee, this time into soft soul. It was based around an obscure silky ballad from 1976 called 'Oh Honey' by a group called Delegation. Despite the mellow vibe and sweet sound, the song was actually about staying up all night to play video games and argue about football with friends as an escape, with the help of herbal relaxants, from the problems of the world. "I'm a massive R&B fan," admitted Dizzee. "Massive. Jodeci, Keith Sweat; all that shit." He laughed when asked whether 'Chillin'...' was his own soundtrack to charming the ladies into bed. "When I was a kid I had my slow jam tapes, of course. Have it ready, man. Ha ha. Would I ever put on one of my own tunes? Nah, that's going a bit far for me!"

The next track, 'Dirtee Cash' (words by Dizzee, music by Cage), was also heavily reliant on a sample, this time from a 1990 number two hit called 'Dirty Cash (Money Talks)' by UK house music crew The Adventures Of Stevie V – so prominent was the sample, in fact, that Dizzee's song almost felt like a cover version. 'Dirtee Cash' was a diatribe aimed at the fame-hungry and the avaricious, the people who spend money they have yet to earn, and our consumerist society that has in turn, suggested Dizzee, created a gun and drug culture. It came complete with a topical reference to the 2008–9 credit crunch, lending the track a newsy feel, echoing the idea, posited by Public Enemy, of rap as a sort of "black CNN" – this was a homegrown version, more like a black ITN. Dizzee told *The Sun* that the song was about "how if you ain't got money, but you still spend it anyway, life is gonna bite you in the arse". It was quite a dark lyric for a Top 10 single – 'Dirtee Cash' was released as the fourth single from *Tongue N' Cheek* on September 21, the same day as the album. His first solo song from the album following the collaborations with Calvin Harris ('Dance Wiv Me' and 'Holiday') and Armand Van Helden ('Bonkers'), it reached number 10 in the charts. A video, directed by W.I.Z. (who had also directed promos for Oasis, Massive Attack, Manic Street Preachers and Primal Scream), was filmed for the single in London. Prepared in four days and shot in five hours next to London's Tower Bridge with a 125-strong cast, the video was an ambitious affair with a dark, carnivalesque atmosphere. It seemingly drew inspiration from Guy Fawkes night, the burning of Joan of Arc and the cult classic 1973 British horror movie *The Wicker Man*. The video featured extras dressed as characters from British history, or holding placards bearing images of icons, from Margaret Thatcher to Princess Diana, while events such as the suffragette movement were alluded to and works of literature – Shakespeare's *The Tempest*, Marx's *Das Kapital*, William Blake's 'Jerusalem' – were burnt, possibly as a comment on the corruption of all values endemic in society. Very dark for a Top 10 single.

The next track on *Tongue N' Cheek*, 'Money, Money', continued the theme of avarice and greed, but it was tempered with a wry self-awareness, alluding to his new-found wealth – the fact was that Dizzee, according to a website called Celebrity Net Worth, was now raking in a cool couple of million pounds a year. Another Dizzee/ Cage team-up, 'Money, Money', boasted about his expensive (£850) jeans and the women who were now flocking to him, although he pre-empted any further criticism that he was being sexist and misogynistic by declaring that he really didn't give a toss what people thought of him. Still, he was at pains to point out that all of his fame and fortune was achieved through considerable effort. Referring to his high-profile 2008 grilling by Jeremy Paxman on *Newsnight*, he drew the distinction between money acquired through hard graft, as in his case, and those who merely accumulated the flash accoutrements of wealth without really deserving to. Dizzee was a contradictory figure in the song, at once ostentatious and prudent, making sure he had a mortgage by the time he was 22 instead of buying shiny rims for his car. But no matter how sensible, he made sure we knew he was not averse to enjoying himself, and in one humorous couplet there was a comparison made between oral gratification and the blowing of a didgeridoo.

Meanwhile, the music was experimental and arrhythmic future dancehall, weird for chart pop but somehow utterly irresistible. The same went for 'Leisure', where the music, composed by Cage and Footsie of Newham Generals, was hard-to-dance-to dance music, albeit music that moved at a titular leisurely pace. It featured all manner of burbles, clicks, taps and production trickery, elaborating a song in which Dizzee boasted in typically insouciant fashion about his couldn't-care-less attitude while paradoxically alluding once more to problems in the ghetto. After penultimate track 'Holiday' came 'Bad Behaviour', with music by Dutch DJ and electronic dance producer Tijs Michiel Verwest, alias Tiësto. 'Bad Behaviour' closed the album on a musical high, with its reprise of a classic anthemic rave to match the coda to 'Holiday'. The lyrics, by contrast, were a low, certainly as far as those who were monitoring Dizzee's songs for sexism were concerned, with its flippant objectification of women. Despite Dizzee's unrepentant ribaldry and advocacy of the carefree superstar life, not to mention a line that managed to make a rhyme out of his wealth and fame with his backside, many, not just parents, were outraged, considering his attitude an obstacle to their enjoyment of the music.

Tongue N' Cheek was an odd mix of social commentary and the "bubblegum nihilism" that critic Simon Reynolds detected in 'Bonkers'. There may have been moments that some found irresponsible ('Road Rage') and overly bawdy and intimate ('Freaky Freaky'), but there was no denying that it was a brilliantly entertaining 40 minutes or so of beats and rhymes, of dance energy and pop hooks. So exuberant was it, such a non-stop cavalcade of bite-sized pop, it was hard to believe that it was made by the same person as *Boy In Da Corner*. And yet it was by far his best album since that epochal début, one that made *Showtime* seem like a retread of the first album and *Maths + English* appear, in retrospect, like a holding exercise. *Tongue N' Cheek*, on the other hand, was a bold, brazen affair, a notion enhanced by the Ben Drury sleeve and its cartoon graffiti typography. In its total embrace of pop but defiant disregard for commercial constraints, it brought a subversive edge to the charts. It was, in many ways, his most 'for real' record, his truest depiction of street life, since *Boy In Da Corner*. It's just that he was aiming his latest music at a broader range of street people, and implied an understanding that many working-class people weren't just content to languish on council estates; that they aspired to better things, such as holidays and pleasure.

"This is probably the album where I've celebrated it most – the high life, living large and just party life in general," he said. "But there's a lot more to me than that." Was he, wondered Tim Adams of *The Observer*, worried about losing touch with the people whose lives he once documented? "If you mean ghetto people," he replied, "then I know exactly how to talk to them, exactly what to say. The way I see it, everyone's looking for a bit of enlightenment, the more outlandish the better. But I want to keep it real with everyone, not just the guys on the estate." He continued: "People say about my first album being raw and gritty but not everyone got it, so I was always trying to be open-minded and branch out. If we're going to talk about hardcore grime and that, they're all basing their whole careers on shit I started eight, nine years ago anyway, let's be real. I ain't taking orders. I don't answer to none of them. It's about making music, innit. That's all it is." Dizzee was simply telling it like he saw it; he was, as Ben Thompson of *The Daily Telegraph* stated, "a journalist at heart, a compulsive observer of his life and times", reporting from the front line of late-Noughties Britain. "It's all reportage," said Dizzee. "I sometimes think I should write a book. I've seen some things, you know, but it's all there in the songs."

Those songs told the truth about contemporary Britain, and if some of them were near the knuckle, then so be it. "People talk about being a good example for the kids," he said, "and putting that perspective out there is the best thing I could do. If you want real truth, I'll tell you real truth, even though I know a lot of people aren't gonna like it." Besides, argued some commentators, by taking centre stage, Dizzee Rascal "was able to make his most radical contribution to British cultural life". He might have been expected to have made that notorious appearance on BBC2's *Newsnight* and behave like a polite, polished young pop star, but that was never the plan. "A lot of people wanted me to go on that show and act super-proper, like I'm grateful to be there," he told Ben Thompson. "I was grateful, but in my own way. I'm not that guy in the suit, speaking the Queen's English. I don't need to be. I can go on *Newsnight* as me. All black people ain't the same: that was the point I wanted to make."

Three months before *Tongue N' Cheek* came out, Michael Jackson died. In a way, Dizzee Rascal was assuming the now vacant position of King of Pop in the affections of the British public, as he told Tim Adams of *The Observer* when the journalist asked how far he believed he could go. "I'm going to be big," he grinned, tongue in cheek, but as ever with a hint that anything was possible, "like Michael Jackson."

CHAPTER 18

Marks Outta Ten

"He's become a beautiful young man. He is established in the musical fabric now in this country and from that point he should be able to do what he likes"

Nick Cage

*T*ongue N' Cheek got a mixed reception from the critics. Many, however, did discern that, despite Dizzee Rascal's pop ambitions, his fourth album was by no means wall-to-wall mainstream pap, containing as it did plenty of music and lyrics every bit as edgy as his startling early grime releases, even if they were surrounded by four hit singles. In fact, the BBC reviewer believed *Tongue N' Cheek* to be "packed with further contenders for Top 10 hits", describing it as a sort of British urban *Thriller*, a reference to Michael Jackson's 50-million-plus-selling Eighties blockbuster, which contained no fewer than seven hit singles. "*Tongue N' Cheek*," it concluded, "is the release to officially crown Dizzee as UK dance/hip hop royalty." Over at Drowned In Sound, the music website took one listen to the album's lyrical content and surmised that "it isn't Dizz's pop music album, it's his pop star album", full as it was of "tales of girls, fast cars and money [that] drip like champagne off a naked thigh." They also noted the "crass sexism and the peacock displays of masculinity", but decided that Dizzee's puckish wit made it all bearable. *Tongue N' Cheek* was, they said, "a vacuous but fun party record". *Slant* magazine was pithy in its assessment: "*Tongue N' Cheek* is Dizzee Rascal's least ambitious and most successfully tasteless album, but whoever said great pop had to be anything more than certifiably junky?" Alexis Petridis at *The Guardian* praised the way Dizzee had achieved his success without having to tone down his lyrics or pop up his sound. The distorted synthesizers on 'Bonkers', for example, were still "edgily thrilling". He was less enamoured of 'Freaky Freaky', whose "nasty and glum" tone made it a sort of grime version of old *Carry On* comedy sexism. And he pointed out the contradiction of admonishing people for their conspicuous consumption while bragging about your huge trainer collection. Nevertheless, the album's highlights, such as 'Bonkers', made the collection "irresistible". The *NME* sadly mourned the death of Dizzee Rascal v 1.0: "It's about time we accepted that the boy in da corner who spat paranoid rage over barrages of digital artillery fire isn't coming back." The new Dizzee was, opined writer Sam Richards, "a bit of a caricature – a clowning psycho, obsessed with cash, gash and acting flash". Still, there were things to enjoy on *Tongue N' Cheek*, from the "brilliantly lairy" 'Money, Money' to 'Bad Behaviour' and its tale of "Dizzee high on champers'n'coke, being noshed off in his speeding Porsche." "Clearly," decided Richards, "this is exactly the kind of pop star we need."

America's Pitchfork saw Dizzee's *Tongue N' Cheek* persona as a logical extension of the "globetrotting good-life playboy" character he sought to portray on *Maths + English*. But what it admired most was the way he leavened this with a "down-to-earth wisdom" that kept his more garish tendencies in check. "*Tongue N' Cheek* [is] a minor inclusion in his catalogue, a quickie that won't make year-end lists like *Boy In Da Corner* and *Showtime* or break new ground for him as a cultural polymath like *Maths + English*," wrote Ian Cohen. "Yet if this is the kind of album he can effortlessly churn out at his leisure, we're in for a promising second decade of the man's work." Pop Matters deduced from the cartoonish cover that *Tongue N' Cheek* was Dizzee Rascal "bidding farewell to the underground that birthed him", and went on to declare the album an "undeniably valiant bid for stardom". In the process, however, he had, they said, "sacrificed a good deal of depth and complexity in the name of accessibility... While *Tongue 'N Cheek* is easily more instantly gratifying than Rascal's previous albums, it lacks the unique perspective and replay value of his more nuanced work."

There were several keen insights and bright ideas about the album from UK music website The Quietus. It divined a difference between Dizzee, a quintessential "cheeky British Herbert", and the thug rappers who dominated the American scene. They noted that 'Dance Wiv Me' was the first 100,000-selling single in the UK since Gnarls Barkley's 'Crazy' in 2006. On 'Freaky Freaky' Dizzee's words clattered out as "a riot of plosive consonance and vocal clicks and tics which create a mass bubble wrap-bursting session of rhymes". 'Chillin Wiv Da Man Dem' was "a blast of bliss hanging in the air like dope smoke on a hot, still summer's day". 'Money, Money' was so close to old-school grime that it "almost could have appeared in a more lo-fi form on *Boy In Da Corner*". Overall, the site decided that "the vast majority" of the songs on *Tongue N 'Cheek* "could easily be released as singles in their own right".

As for *The Daily Telegraph*, it noted that, "From the green fields of Glastonbury to the dance floors of Ibiza", Dizzee's 'Bonkers' had been the "standout tune of the summer". As a consequence, *Tongue N' Cheek* found him "in party mood, ready to celebrate the leisure society and its hedonistic culture of cash and consumerism". The album also signalled the emergence of a new kind of pop music, the paper determined, one that Dizzee Rascal almost singlehandedly invented: grime-inflected urban pop. "He has paved the way for an invasion of the Top 40 by a series of improbably named characters [such as] Tinchy Stryder, Wiley and Chipmunk." Apart from the fact that Wiley was originally Dizzee's mentor (although Dizzee arguably created the space for Wiley to achieve wider acceptance), this assertion was accurate: Dizzee's success with the singles from *Tongue N' Cheek* allowed a slew of new, young grime-pop acts to colonise the UK charts, to the extent that, by summer 2010, Paul MacInnes, in his coverage for *The Guardian* of the Glastonbury festival, could declare that "urban is the new pop". Artists such as Tinie Tempah, Roll Deep, N-Dubz, Professor Green and the aforementioned Tinchy and Chipmunk all enjoyed huge Top 10 hits in Dizzee's wake. "Last year," wrote Macinnes, "the press stopped calling Dizzee a rapper; he was now a pop star." But what had really changed, he said, was not Dizzee's status but people's taste, with the likes of Tinie Tempah and Roll Deep (both then with recent number ones), as well as N-Dubz and Chipmunk, now "virtual fixtures on Radio 1".

But how was all this success and attendant fame affecting Dizzee? "Parts of me are still the same person as back then," he said, comparing himself now, in the late Noughties, to his earlier, grime-ier self, adding, "but I'm older and my situation's different." But then, as he told *Clash* magazine, he'd grown accustomed to being famous, having been a celebrity ever since he won the Mercury Music Prize in 2003. "The Mercury award was worldwide fame," he said. "I still had paparazzi outside my house. How I dealt with it was by getting on with my work." Besides, he explained that he was now a changed man, and that he was less prone to getting into trouble than when he was 18. "I'm an adult now, man. It's more and more about the music for me."

And yet, for his supporters, it was his character as much as his music that was his unique selling point, hence the legions of fans who would approach him in the street. "It's been mad," he said. "Being recognised by people in the street that you wouldn't think would recognise you. To be fair, it's mostly loads of love, man. All love. It's nice that people are enjoying it." Dizzee got some sense of how much people were now enjoying him, and of how many of them there were, when he appeared at the Glastonbury Festival in June 2009. There, he performed a medley of hits by the man whom he had supplanted as Britain's unofficial King of Pop – Michael Jackson, who died just as the festival began. During his Pyramid Stage slot, he rapped over 'That's Not My Name' by indie electro duo The Ting Tings and M.I.A.'s 'Paper Planes' before declaring, "We lost a legend this week, so I think we should do something to remember him." His DJ, Semtex, proceeded to play snippets of Jackson's hits, including 'Billie Jean' and 'Thriller'. Dizzee also performed a selection of his own hits, both old and brand new, from 'Fix Up, Look Sharp' to 'Holiday', and indulged in some crowd participation. For the climax, the audience went bonkers to 'Bonkers'.

"When I'm on Glastonbury main stage in front of 90,000 people, that's when I stand there and think, 'This is what it's about, man'," he said with a happy sigh. "Of course there are days when I just want to be left alone, when I want to have a day off. It's tough, innit. But I accept it now. I walk down the street and think, 'Fuck it, man, it's lovely.'" He said at the end of his interview with *Clash* magazine that there remained one ambition unfulfilled. "I still haven't had a number one album," he said. "Platinum, maybe double-platinum, number one around the world consecutively. That'd be good."

One downside of fame, he admitted to Tim Adams of *The Observer*, was the complications that resulted from all the attention he was now receiving from females. It was during his V Festival appearance at the end of August (see Chapter 16) that Adams saw the rapping pop star besieged by girls – "many in curious fancy dress: a mad hatter, a Wonder Woman" – which forced him to take cover in his trailer. Was Dizzee, wondered Adams, beginning to see the value of settling (down) with one woman, notwithstanding the profligate attitude expressed in tracks such as 'Freaky Freaky', where it seemed too many was never enough? "I've loved a few girls," he revealed. "But then you get mixed up between love and lust, or I do anyway. But then every time I think I want to settle down a bit, I think... nah. There's too many..."

Despite his burgeoning reputation as a playboy, he claimed not to be as much of a clubber as before. "You don't see me out in the West End that much," he said. He'd done his time hanging about with footballers and other glitterati, and he'd had his fill. "I've done that, but to be honest it's not always that much of a good time."

He would rather stay at home, he said, "playing computer games or making music." According to his manager, Nick Cage, it was Dizzee's commitment to recording and performing that set him apart from many of his peers, for whom the lure of lucre and the trappings of fame were far more important than the music that put them in the position to enjoy them in the first place. Dizzee could so easily have become one of them. "He could have become an arsehole, given his journey, but he hasn't," said Cage. "He's become a beautiful young man. He is established in the musical fabric now in this country and from that point he should be able to do what he likes. If he wants to do a 15th-century chamber music album – and I wouldn't put it past him – well, all right, bring it on. He's doing it because it hurts if he doesn't do it. He knows the alternative."

It wasn't exactly 15th-century chamber music, but it wasn't far off when Dizzee appeared onstage in his "James Bond suit" complete with bow tie (which he bought for the occasion in Harrods), alongside Dame Shirley Bassey for a performance of John Barry's 007 classic 'Diamonds Are Forever' at London's Royal Albert Hall for the Children In Need concert on November 12, 2009. The conductor's face when Dizzee came onstage for his cameo two minutes into the song was worth the price of admission alone.

Restlessly inventive and ever keen to finesse his material, in autumn 2009 Dizzee worked up an alternative version of *Tongue N' Cheek*, which featured a bonus disc entitled *Foot N' Mouth* that came free with the album when purchased from HMV stores. The extra disc comprised a single track, lasting 27 minutes and 54 seconds. It was a podcast that included an introduction, various skits and snippets of songs, interviews by DJ Semtex with Dirtee Stank signings Newham Generals and Smurfie Syco, and Dizzee Rascal talking about a forthcoming Dirtee Stank project called 'Maniac Music'. There was a further iteration of *Tongue N' Cheek: Mistletoe N' Wine (Xmas Edition)*, which was released through iTunes just in time for Christmas 2009. This version of the album featured 10 bonus tracks (six remixes, by up-and-coming names such as Burns, plus the videos for 'Bonkers', 'Holiday', 'Dance Wiv Me' and 'Dirtee Cash').

In what was becoming an annual tradition, Dizzee ended 2009 with a Q&A in *The Guardian* (the previous year's one saw him asked, "To whom would you most like to say 'sorry', and why?", to which he replied, "To my mum, for being such a fucker when I was little"). He announced that he would be touring Australia in January 2010, and going on the road with Lily Allen in February. There would be a further single lifted from *Tongue N' Cheek*, but there wouldn't be another album for the foreseeable future (although there would, in summer 2010, be yet another version of *T N' C*, this one featuring several brand new tracks). "I'll never run out of things to rap about," he said. "Sometimes you sit there and think, 'I can't do it, I can't do it.' Then something happens and you start writing." He talked about collaborations – apparently Rolf Harris had expressed a desire to work with him – and named The Prodigy as the band with whom he'd most like to record. He was asked, in the light of his appearance on *Newsnight*, whether he would like to go on BBC1's *Question Time*, to which he responded by saying, "I'm sure I could make it an entertaining show. I'd bring up all the world's events and laugh at them, like *The Harry Hill Show*." As it was Christmas, and given his popularity with women, he was asked "how many girls he was planning to get off with under the mistletoe at Christmas using the opening gambit, 'Izzy, wizzy, let's have a kissee for Dizzee?'", which flummoxed even him. And as for any "bonkers New Year's resolutions"? "Yeah," he joked. "Waste less time. Party more. And fuck you! Ha!"

It was also a time of sober reflection. Because it was the end, not just of the year but of the Noughties as well, there was a slew of journalists queuing up to quiz Dizzee about the highs and lows of his decade. His personal highlight, he said, was reaching number one for the first time, with 'Dance Wiv Me'. "All the work I'd been doing started to make sense for me at that point," he said. The low point was getting stabbed six times in Ayia Napa. "That," he said, understandably, "was pretty shit." The greatest losses as far as he was concerned, in a decade that saw countless musicians pass away, were Michael Jackson and James Brown. The one thing he would change if he could about the era was the credit crunch. His greatest hope for the next 10 years was "to be making better music than I'm making now, and to grow as a better man". And his proudest moment was "becoming a national treasure, firmly implanted into music history". The thing that made him the angriest was, he said with a snarl, "The fucking music industry – it's full of poseurs and dickheads and people who don't know what they are talking about." And if he had to sum up the period in three words, he would pick, "Exciting and productive – I've actually been a part of it in a really big way."

Meanwhile, *Boy In Da Corner* was voted top in many end-of-decade critics' polls, and *Observer Music Monthly* anointed Dizzee its Pop Star Of The Decade. He was delighted with the news. "I'm enjoying reaching people no one would've expected me to reach, considering where I've come from, and the music I started out making," he said. "It shows what's possible, and it inspires people – and not just people from the same background as me, either." And then, in *The Observer* newspaper, in a survey of the decade's cultural landmarks, from cinema to art to television, Dizzee Rascal was chosen as the representative of the world of music. "Like all the most pivotal musicians," the paper wrote, "Dizzee transcended genre. He documented the fears, loves, mishaps and misdemeanours of young Bow with an unsparing eye, in another league to all the MCs around him. Interviewed in the wake of Obama's election win, he made Jeremy Paxman look foolish on *Newsnight*. He wasn't scared of looking foolish either, pogoing in a shark costume in the video for his number one hit 'Bonkers'. He sounded like the decade: fast, vexed and funny."

The way the last 10 years had gone for him, who would bank on Dizzee Rascal not having as successful a second decade of the 21st century as the first?

CHAPTER 19

Bonkers

"The chance to do a disco tune came up so I grabbed it. I like to fuck around with different types of music, going where the mood takes me. When it feels right, I do it, off the cuff."

Dizzee Rascal

Having conquered the UK, Dizzee turned his attention towards the rest of the world in early 2010. In January, he travelled to Australia for its nationwide Big Day Out festival. He had already done the BDO in 2008 and was honoured to be invited back; Australia, in turn, was delighted to see him again. "The Australian vibe is wicked, man! I love coming here for the Big Day Out, it's a brilliant tour," he told music website In The Mix. He compared the respective live atmospheres back home and down under. "Australia and UK vibes are quite similar in following and response," he said. "That's why I'm surprised; even so far away it's quite awesome. The vibe of the show, the people are beautiful – they just move like mad, and that's kind of what I'm going for." Far from allowing all the adulation to go to his head, however, Dizzee insisted he was bowled over to be so adored so far from home. "I just love that my music's reached Australia, it's something that I never even fathomed. I'm happy, man." Discussing his music, he stated that the prime motivation for his fourth album, *Tongue N' Cheek*, had been "partying and having a good time." His mission, he said, was to "make music that moves people, physically as well as emotionally". He didn't believe his approach had changed that much over the years. "The emphasis is still on the rapping. I'm just trying to get people to dance and have a good time, especially on this album. I have some social issues, but the main reason is to make people have a good time."

At the Mt Smart Stadium in Auckland on January 15 the reaction to 'Bonkers' was so overwhelming that a local newspaper wrote: "It provided one of those Big Day Out moments that will be talked about for years to come." In Sydney, Dizzee was apparently "a revelation", and got the 40,000 or so sweating revellers bouncing in unison to his uniquely British hip hop in the sweltering Aussie heat. The way Dizzee, his hype man and his DJ whipped up the crowd into a frenzy of mass participation was like nothing the locals had seen since the heyday of Rage Against The Machine in the Nineties. The show in Melbourne saw Dizzee create a fun party atmosphere, even if his between-song banter did perplex some, one local journalist joking that she needed a dictionary to translate some of his colloquial chatter. But there was no misunderstanding the audience's mood – the charismatic performer had them wrapped around his little finger. The crowd at Brisbane, where he was joined by Lily Allen and Calvin Harris, was considerably smaller, at around 5,000, but still both the hits and lesser-known album tracks, old and new, were rapturously received, the punters' vigorous shimmying creating a dust cloud that was clearly visible from a distance.

It was while he was on tour in Australia that Dizzee recorded an anniversary tribute to *Newsnight* on the occasion of the BBC2 news review show's 30th birthday. Jeremy Paxman's favourite hip hop interviewee – who was famously featured on the programme after Barack Obama won the US presidential election, and then incorporated the programme's theme tune for the intro to his 2009 Glastonbury set – was caught on camera in the beautiful sunshine, wearing shades and a Nirvana T-shirt, declaring to the camera, "Many years of continued success to you and your crew. Respect!"

It wasn't all glad tidings down under. During his BDO gig in Sydney, while he was being interviewed by reporter Alison Stephenson for Australian website www.news.au, their light-hearted conversation suddenly took a turn for the dark. Stephenson asked him about how he had once fallen over on stage. "Yeah, yeah, I have stacked it on stage," said Dizzee, but when Stephenson continued to probe him about the incident – "So you didn't eat the floor or anything like that?" she enquired – he became defensive, even aggressive. "What the fuck do you want from me, man, I've already said I done it. Yeah, I stacked it, bitch. Fuck!" The interview ended abruptly and Dizzee headed back to his trailer. Stephenson didn't give the matter too much thought thereafter until all the other reporters and publicists approached her and demanded that she return to the media area, since Dizzee was apparently refusing to do any more press unless the video of his "less than polite" interview with Stephenson was destroyed. With so many interviews lined up for the day, Stephenson had to be escorted over to Dizzee's trailer, where he was in high dudgeon, and sign a document agreeing that the footage be scrapped. "A publicist came running up to me declaring I had to go back to the media area immediately and my Dizzee Rascal interview had to be deleted," said Stephenson. "I was escorted to Dizzee's trailer so his UK manager and publicist could emerge, watch me sign the document and agree to just forget about it and move on. All I was told was: 'Dizzee wasn't happy with it'." The Big Day Out publicist, Miranda Brown, declined to comment.

Back in Britain a few weeks later, any bad feelings left by the Australian incident were forgotten when, on February 16, at the 30th annual Brit Awards, Dizzee Rascal won in the Best British Male category. Dressed in his smart James Bond suit, he also provided one of the highlights of the ceremony when he joined new British singing sensation Florence And The Machine (who won the Best British Album award for *Lungs*) for a mini-medley of his *Tongue N' Cheek* track 'Dirtee Cash' and 'You Got The Love', a soul/disco tune from 1991 by Candi Staton and The Source that Florence Welch had recorded for solo release in 2009, and with which she had charted at number five in November of that year. The Dizzee/Florence 'mash-up', entitled 'You Got The Dirtee Love', performed live at the Brits, was one of the few standout moments at the 2010 ceremony.

It was a significant performance in many ways − recorded live at 9pm on February 16, by 2am the following morning − Wednesday February 17 − the live recording of 'You Got The Dirtee Love' was on sale exclusively via iTunes, with all proceeds from the single going towards the Brit Trust. There was plenty of money generated: on February 21, the single entered the UK charts at number two − higher than Welch's own version, and two places higher than Candi Staton's original. By May 10, it had been certified silver, with sales in excess of 280,000. The day after the Brits, Oliver Schusser, senior director of iTunes Europe, said: "We're delighted to give iTunes customers the chance to download an amazing live track from Florence And The Machine and Dizzee Rascal, just hours after their performance at the Brits last night." Dizzee and Florence's 'You Got The Dirtee Love' would become one of the ubiquitous hits of the year, ever-present on daytime radio, while the pair, the biggest male and female pop stars in Britain (give or take Robbie Williams, Amy Winehouse and Lily Allen), would repeat their Brits duet several more times that summer, at Radio 1's Big Weekend in North Wales in May and several times at Glastonbury in June. Indeed, Alexis Petridis joked in his Glastonbury festival overview in *The Guardian* that it was part of "a blitzkrieg campaign to make [the song] the omnipresent soundtrack of this year's festival" following Florence's own version of it on the main stage, her duet with Dizzee on the Pyramid stage, and her performance of it the next day with indie band The XX on the John Peel Stage. "You start to wonder," commented Petridis, "if those people peering trepidatiously into the lavatories before using them are concerned about hygiene, or just terrified she will be in there as well."

In March 2010, Dizzee teamed up with another female pop star, Lily Allen, for some arena dates. "The *enfants terribles* of the music scene", as website All Gigs described them – or "the voices of their generation" as they were termed rather more politely in *The Daily Telegraph* – co-headlined shows at Manchester Arena on March 5 and at London's O2 Arena on March 7. This was their first endeavour together since Allen's collaboration with Dizzee on the track 'Wanna Be' from his 2007 album, *Maths+ English*. At Manchester the *NME* reviewer Rick Martin was surprised and disappointed that Dizzee and Lily didn't do a duet, surprised because, as he wrote, "At the moment Dizzee's so obsessed with calculated collaborations that you have to wonder whether he'd record a version of 'Summer Holiday' with Cliff Richard if it pushed him even further from his grime roots into the bosom of pop enormity." The only guest artists on both acts' stages were "Britrap goon" Professor Green for a drum'n'bass version of Allen's number one 'Smile', and reality TV loser Daniel Pearce, who had fared badly, not once but twice, on *Popstars: The Rivals* and *The X Factor*, and who provided backing vocals for Dizzee. Martin was less than impressed with the "dozen or so mostly unnecessary session players, including a guitarist probably borrowed from a Whitesnake tribute band" who "fretwanks during every breakdown". Nor did he enjoy the "ill-conceived" version of Nirvana's 'Smells Like Teen Spirit'. Nevertheless, noted Martin, "Dylan Mills [looked] every inch the king of all he surveys, with his sights set still further."

The 02 Arena show was rather better, according to Hazel Sheffield of *The Daily Telegraph*, or at least she responded more favourably to the performances of the numerous auxiliary musicians who joined Dizzee onstage. "[Dizzee] greeted the full arena with the swagger of a man primed for the challenge of entertaining thousands," she declared. "Big-budget production afforded him an expansive backing band including rock guitarists, who came into their own on samples of Nirvana's 'Teen Spirit', soulful backing singers, a brass section and his tour DJ, Semtex, whose noisy basslines squelched around the rafters and had everyone bouncing in the pit." Dizzee, meanwhile, acquitted himself with "magnetic insouciance". Allen's performance, by contrast, was marred by a huge fight that broke out metres from the stage, and she left in tears, contributing to "an undeniably stilted performance". Where "Dizzee Rascal stood tall, reminding everybody of his remarkable ascendancy", Allen seemed strangely muted as she bid farewell to the music industry, amid claims that she had had enough of the limelight and wanted to start a family.

Dizzee Rascal and Lily Allen were both in the news again in April when they were each nominated for prestigious Ivor Novello awards for songwriting excellence. Allen was named in two categories, both for her number one single 'The Fear', while Dizzee was nominated for the Best Contemporary Song (for 'Bonkers') and Album (for *Tongue N' Cheek*) awards, where he was up against La Roux, Bat For Lashes, Paolo Nutini and *The Duckworth Lewis Method*, the album by ex-Divine Comedy frontman Neil Hannon and Thomas Walsh. The awards were held on May 20 and this time it was Allen who emerged victorious, winning in both categories for which she had been nominated. Dizzee, however, despite turning up suited and booted and having his photograph taken smiling with *The Daily Mirror*'s gossip-hungry '3am Girls', left empty-handed.

Dizzee was probably too busy to care. At the end of the month, on May 31, 2010, he and Dirtee Stank re-released the album *Tongue N' Cheek* with a whole CD of extra material. This was an expanded version, rebranded the *Dirtee Deluxe Edition* and issued to celebrate *Tongue N' Cheek* going platinum. It included the original album plus five remixes and live versions, and five brand new tracks. The first track on the new CD of additional material was 'Dirtee Disco', which, on May 23, when it was released as a digital download, became the fifth single to be lifted from *Tongue N' Cheek* (or at least, the new version of same). It featured the former *X Factor* contestant Daniel Pearce, who had joined Dizzee for his recent MEN and 02 dates, and sampled the already much-covered 1972 tune by The Staple Singers, 'I'll Take You There'.

It also became his fourth number one (his fifth if you include the Band Aid 20 single) – as a result, Dizzee now had the record for the most number one singles on an album by a solo male artist. Not everyone was pleased with his full-blown immersion in the world of flared trousers and open-necked shirts, one portrayed most famously in the John Travolta movie *Saturday Night Fever*. Robert Copsey of the Digital Spy blog was quite negative in his two-star review: "'Dirtee Disco' is a Seventies-influenced party tune on which Dizz raps about doing the robot, drinking JD & Coke and wrapping his hands around the nearest girl's waist over some oh-so-groovy beats. It's more likely to remind you of your local Flares nightclub than the hedonistic heyday of Studio 54. Close to the start of the track, Dizz warns: 'If you can't say something nice, then keep quiet.' We'd better keep our lips firmly shut, then."

As ever, Dizzee was unrepentant: "It's just like a massive party record, a massive summer tune. It does what it says on the tin," he told the BBC's *Newsbeat* programme. He added in the *NME*, when it asked if he'd "gone disco" for 2010: "I've not gone disco totally, man, it's just for this song. The chance to do a disco tune came up so I grabbed it. I like to fuck around with different types of music, going where the mood takes me. When it feels right, I do it, off the cuff."

The music video for 'Dirtee Disco' took place in a local village hall, where sexagenarian 'DJ Derek' entertained a bunch of elderly revellers with his mobile disco. Dizzee's arrival on the scene, gorgeous girls in tow, inevitably got the party started, transforming the hall into a den of iniquity and rambunctious dancing. "There's no *Saturday Night Fever* influence," he insisted in the *NME*. "That's not John Travolta strutting, that's me, wearing a £2,000 Gucci suit. The moves are more influenced by *You Don't Mess With The Zohan* [a 2008 comedy starring Adam Sandler]." He added: "Keep an eye out for the models – I chose them. The video's about being able to have a good time wherever you go, whether it's a club or a church hall."

Of the other brand new songs on the second CD of the *Dirtee Deluxe Edition* of *Tongue N' Cheek*, 'Nuffin' Long' revisited the rampant juvenilia of 'Freaky Freaky', a tale of casual sex that rhymed "long" with "thong", while the upbeat skank-pop sounded like a Lily Allen backing track. 'Marks Outta Ten' was equally leering and salacious, a song in which Dizzee spies his prey in a club and decides, over a straight house rhythm, that she will be the lucky recipient of his charms that night. The reference to his potential companion's unattractive acquaintance and the line drawing the distinction between love and cold, hard sex provided more grist to the mill of those who believed Dizzee was mired in misogyny. In spite of this, some reviewers believed it to be a viable future single. 'Heavy', a collaboration with the highly regarded drum'n'bass team Chase & Status, was better received, especially by grime die-hards who considered it far superior to "all that cheesy disco nonsense" he'd been purveying of late.

"Seriously, 'Heavy' is the biggest tune Dizzee has spat on for ages," commented one writer. "Far from sordid disco, house and all the other shit Dizzee has been dipping his shit in these past years. He should go back to grime and heavy basslines. Period." The last of the brand new compositions was 'Doin' It Big', recorded with Newham Generals, offering a compromise between Dizzee's grime lothario persona and some serious dark electro action. Notwithstanding any misgivings about the lyrics, these five new tracks came impressively hot on the heels of the *Tongue N' Cheek* material and were musically strong team-ups with Nick Cage, Chase & Status and Footsie of Newham Generals, offering several pointers as to Dizzee's next step.

In addition there were five further tracks on the *Deluxe Edition*: 'You Got The Dirtee Love', featuring Florence Welch and recorded live at the Brit Awards in February 2010; a version of 'Brand New Day' recorded live at the BBC Electric Proms 2009; 'Fix Up, Look Sharp' recorded live at the BBC Electric Proms 2009; and remixes of 'Bonkers' (by Doorly) and 'Holiday' (by Laidback Luke). Online magazine First Up was particularly taken with the last track, voicing the opinions of many grime fans when its reviewer wrote: "Hopefully, Dizzee's done with house and disco and bad dance music that he left those grime roots behind in favour for. It's time to go back, back to them heavy basslines and spitting fire. I cross my fingers, cos even if Dizzee's razor-sharp lyrical ability and wit remain at the core of his sound, this dance routine is getting old and tired."

It was probably safe to say, then, that said reviewer wouldn't have been overly keen on what Dizzee Rascal did next.

CHAPTER 20

Shout

"I'm dedicating my life to improving the mood. I'm bringing up the general happiness of the country."

Dizzee Rascal

Dizzee Rascal made some unexpected and/or unusual appearances in print, TV and radio throughout 2009 and early 2010. He performed a version of 'Bonkers' on BBC2's *Later…With Jools Holland* in September 2009 with a live drummer, a sit-down acoustic guitarist and a stand-up bassist (borrowed from trip hop group Massive Attack) that made the song sound more like a hoedown than a grime beatdown – there were even some "yee-haws!" discernible at one point. Just as odd was his version of 'Holiday' on the same edition of the show, which, with its Spanish guitar, had a distinctly Castilian feel. In January, he sat in for presenter Zane Lowe, as the latter took a break from his Radio 1 show ahead of Dizzee's Australian Big Day Out adventure, and for some that might have seemed surprising, being on an indie rock programme, albeit one with a history of playing dance and grime.

While he was in Brisbane, he made a sensationalist appearance in a local newspaper under the hold-the-front-page banner headline

'Dizzee Rascal Goes Bonkers In Australia', after he allegedly "tried to grab an audience member" for, bizarrely, throwing a stick of deodorant at him during his gig. According to an *NME* report, Dizzee halted his set mid-song, jumped into the photographers' pit and attempted to wrestle with a blond-haired man in the audience, whom other fans were pushing towards the stage barrier. Luckily, security intervened and prevented a fracas.

In May 2010 there was a story about him in the *News Of The World's* Celeb XS showbiz pages entitled 'One's Bonkers'. Next to a mocked-up image of Prince William wearing a hoodie and a bling crucifix, it was reported that the heir to the throne had been getting in on the act following Dizzee's encounter with Prince Harry in July 2009 at the 02 Wireless Festival in Hyde Park (see Chapter 16) and had helicoptered into Radio 1's Big Weekend festival in Bangor, Wales, just to see his favourite rapper. With his girlfriend, Kate Middleton, in tow, he stood at the side of the stage during Dizzee's duet with Florence And The Machine of 'You Got The Dirtee Love', mouthing all the words to the song. Afterwards, His Royal Shyness tentatively approached the rapper for a chat. "Dizzee was dumbstruck," said a *NOTW* source. "Wills told him he would try playing his tunes at Buckingham Palace." Dizzee was tickled pink at the notion of The Queen shouting at her grandson to "turn that racket down". "The whole thing," said the source," was a sight to behold."

Even more of a sight to behold was his appearance on the final of ITV's *Britain's Got Talent*, on Saturday June 5, with *Gavin & Stacey* star James Corden. It was their first performance of 'Shout For England', England's unofficial World Cup anthem that the rapper and the comedian had recently recorded for release on June 13. A mash-up of Tears For Fears' 1984 hit 'Shout' and Nineties R&B nugget 'No Diggity' by swingbeat pioneer Teddy Riley's group Blackstreet, the money raised from the single was to go to Great Ormond Street Hospital, with both Dizzee and Corden waiving their royalties from the song. It was an interactive affair, with England fans invited to contribute to the song by singing the chorus – alongside Corden and Rascal via a free phone line. During the song, Dizzee urged footballers Wayne Rooney, Steven Gerrard et al to do what no England team had done since 1966 and win the World Cup. He also suggested that the players set aside ego battles (an allusion, perhaps, to the off-pitch activities of the likes of Ashley Cole and John Terry and their associated tabloid sex scandals) and leave their WAGs at home to focus on the beautiful game.

A story in *The Sun* revealed that *Britain's Got Talent* and *Pop Idol* entrepreneur Simon Cowell, who issued the single on his SyCo label (in association with the telecommunications company TalkTalk), had "been sitting on this song for 15 years", waiting for the right moment to release it. With Dizzee and Corden on board, the project finally had been given the green light. "It has been a long, slow and painful labour," said a *Sun* source, looking ahead to the *Britain's Got Talent* finale. "Now the lads [Dizzee and Corden] are under serious pressure to be ready in time for their big performance in front of more than 10 million viewers at the weekend."

The duo's début performance of 'Shout For England' on *Britain's Got Talent* saw Dizzee the first to emerge from behind a giant England flag wearing a white England shirt emblazoned with a red number one and red letters spelling out his name, as well as a red cap and a pair of baggy khaki shorts. He immediately launched into his rallying cry, designed to put a rocket up the England team's collective backside. Then Corden, in a red England shirt, emerged with a barmy army of England fans, seemingly hundreds of them flooding the stage, chanting and waving flags as rapper and comedian traded deliberately clunky dance moves. It was by turns rousing and ridiculous, and depending on your vantage point either spine-tingling or blind jingoism. Still, it served its purpose, because within days 'Shout For England' was at the top of the charts, making it Dizzee's sixth number one (including the Band Aid 20 project in 2004). It débuted at number one based on download sales alone, ironically beating 'Frisky' by Dizzee acolyte Tinie Tempah to the top slot, as well as another World Cup song, 'Wavin' Flag (The Celebration Mix),' by K'Naan. 'Shout For England' sold more than 100,000 copies in its first chart week despite only being available for four days (the downloadable version of the track was released on Wednesday, and the UK chart surveys the period from Sunday to Saturday). The song spent a second week at pole position on June 20, and was finally knocked off the top the week after by Katy Perry's 'California Gurls'.

While some saw Dizzee's football song and appearance on Britain's favourite talent show as the ultimate examples of him selling out, others warmed to this, the latest instalment in his ongoing transformation from marginal cult hero to national treasure. *The Daily Telegraph* was so moved by the *Britain's Got Talent* performance that it ran an article entitled "Why we love Dizzee". It asserted that, while most football songs – such as "the execrable Spice Girls effort for France '98" – were routinely dreadful, 'Shout For England' was made more than acceptable by dint of Dizzee's "cheek and charm". The newspaper went on to praise his appearance that same week at the Capital Radio Summertime Ball held at Wembley Stadium, where Dizzee stole the show with his energetic renditions of 'Dirtee Disco', 'Bonkers' and 'You Got The Dirtee Love' with Florence And The Machine, which infected the stadium with joyous abandon. "Even up against US tween phenomenon Justin Bieber and bionic pop princess Rihanna," wrote the *Telegraph*, "the loudest screams of the 70,000 Wembley Stadium crowd were reserved for the rapper, once more sporting his England top. Even the mums and dads who had been dragged along by their children loved his rendition of knockabout hits 'Bonkers' and 'Holiday'." The newspaper described him as "a sort of 21st-century Del Boy – he has updated the archetype of the roguish Cockney chancer for multicultural Britain, his Ghanaian heritage far less relevant to our national sense of who he is than his origins in Bow, east London and his vivid, memorable wordplay." It celebrated his "cocky attitude and quick, instinctive wit", which it found "endearing", and decided that he had made British rap a viable genre after years in the shadow of the more radical, innovative American variety. And it hailed the "seismic shift" that he had effected in the pop landscape: "Today, the charts are swelled with an army of Dizzee Rascal acolytes and imitators whose names – Tinie Tempah, Tinchy Stryder – echo the cartoonish, playful feel of their avatar's...

Far from the discordant grime sound that Dizzee first popularised, their music, like his current output, is accomplished urban pop." And yet, despite the legions of mini-mes, they concluded, there was only one Dizzee. "He remains unique. Like Dalí advertising Alka Seltzer, his personal brand is undiminished by his football song: it's the mark of a true artistic star that, whatever format they turn their hand to, their credibility remains intact."

That same month, men's monthly magazine *GQ* ran a feature defending Dizzee Rascal from the naysayers who considered him a sell-out and a misogynist, one who had betrayed the original grime cause. Critics may have preferred his early "tales of alienation and urban blight" rather than the piña colada/rather/lager rhyme scheme of 'Holiday', but *GQ* readers were reminded that much of his early work, especially *Showtime* – which "has been airbrushed out of Dizzee's career trajectory like one of Stalin's foes" – failed to sell. Going against the cognoscenti grain, the magazine proclaimed *Maths + English* and *Tongue N' Cheek* his best work to date, saying: "He is someone who gets better with age – whether it's the shameless pop of 'Bonkers' or the more dramatic social consciousness material such as 'Sirens'." As for being an appalling sexist, it acknowledged the difficulty of defending some of his more risqué lyrics and agreed that he did have songs, such as 'Freaky Freaky', that were unarguably, incredibly sexist; nevertheless, they were also – "rather awkwardly," *GQ* added as an aside – "great party records", reminding readers that "one inconvenient truth is that some of the best hip hop is sexist". And besides, who could argue against a following such as the one accrued by Dizzee Rascal, with whom "the whole country wants to sing along"?

Whether for or against Dizzee Rascal, a defender of his new direction or a detractor, there was no denying that he had an ear for a hit record, not to mention an eye for talent, even if he had yet to prove himself in an A&R capacity (none of his Dirtee Stank signings had yet made much of a commercial mark). And so it made sense that, in June, he was signed up to be one of the judges on the panel for Sky 1 HD's new talent search programme, *Must Be The Music*, which was set to air in August 2010. "The golden boy of the British music scene, Dizzee Rascal," announced Sky's press office, "will be joined by multiple award-winning singer and pianist Jamie Cullum and chart-topping singer/songwriter Sharleen Spiteri." Hosted by the ubiquitous Fearne Cotton, the show was to be filmed throughout the summer as the search began for the UK's best new music act – and there were to be no age or style restrictions, so it could be a gospel choir, an indie rock band, a rapper or a soprano singer. "Its unique new format hands back control to the artists themselves, empowered by creative support, promotional advice and a cash fund of £100,000 to kick-start their career," ran the press release, explaining that the final would be held live at "one of the UK's biggest and most famous music venues", where the finalists would be asked to perform on the same stage as the show's judges. Dizzee, the post-grime Simon Cowell, was just the man for the job, although it was not known if he would be as hard to please as the high-trousered entrepreneur, or if he would be more of a Cheryl Cole-style pushover. "I know how hard it is to break into the music industry," he said, "and I am giving all you fellow musicians out there a chance to come and show me, the other judges and the rest of the UK that we really do have some of the best musicians in the world right under our noses, who deserve a break. I'm here to give you that break."

Dizzee received another great accolade in June when he became one of the 'Listed Londoners' on Robert Elms' excellent daily BBC Radio London lunchtime show. As a Listed Londoner, he was given the opportunity – afforded to such varied and esteemed previous Listed Londoners as comedian Rik Mayall and Madonna producer William Orbit – the opportunity to discuss his preferred (and least loved) aspects of the capital, from his favourite day out to his most loved or hated building on the London skyline. Elms also took the opportunity to reflect back on Dizzee's brilliant career, following his journey from underground grime hopeful to household-name pop sensation.

Dizzee's household-name status meant that his appearance at the Glastonbury festival at the end of June 2010 was certain to be triumphant, and it was. Introducing the coverage of his Friday-night performance, followed by that of notorious US rapper Snoop Dogg, BBC3 presenters Reggie Yates and Edith Bowman warned viewers to expect "some very strong language coming from both their potty mouths".

In the summer late-evening light, Dizzee's arrival onstage – in the slot between Vampire Weekend and headliners Gorillaz – wearing a white number 10 England shirt, beige shorts and chunky white trainers, was met by a tumultuous cheer from the crowd. Watched from the side of the stage by friends, family, journalists and several musicians, including Seasick Steve and Alex Turner of Arctic Monkeys, he launched into 'Shout For England', two days ahead of the squad's match against Germany (which they subsequently lost 4–1). His facility with a large audience was now evident for all to see as he led the assembled thousands, on the hottest day of the year so far, in a chorus of the song's "come and have a go if you think you're hard enough" refrain. 'Jus' A Rascal' was next, complete with hard-rock guitars, Dizzee joined onstage by a full band, including two long-haired types resembling renegades from a grunge or boogie band. 'Holiday' followed, during which Dizzee exhorted the crowd to "bounce bounce bounce!" The transition at the end of the song transformed Glastonbury into one enormous rave, and appropriately induced a state of ecstasy in the throng. He played his perennial crowd-pleasing mash-up of 'Stand Up Tall' and Nirvana's 'Smells Like Teen Spirit', before Florence Welch made her predictable guest appearance, her flaming red hair offset by a sheer black dress, for 'You Got The Dirtee Love'. Florence kissed Dizzee at the end of a short but exhilarating set, after which Glastonbury experienced 'Bonkers' madness. "Put your hands in the air!" shouted Bow's best-known son after his biggest hit. "Dizzee Rascal Glastonbury 2010, you know what fuckin' time it is!" There was total mania as he turned a field in Somerset into a sweaty inner-city club. There was something more than a little heart-warming about the creator of one of the most avant-garde and extreme slabs of noise of the early 21st century becoming the biggest pop star in the country. Dizzee just took it all in his stride: "Yeah, latuh!" he grinned, and he was gone.

After the gig, Dizzee was interviewed by Bowman and Yates. Bowman described it as "an amazing performance", joking that he and Florence ought to get married. Yates asked him about his expectations for the gig compared to the previous year, since which time his popularity had grown several-fold following four number one hits. Dizzee felt that it went better than Glastonbury 2009. He also said that he had been watching Snoop backstage, anxiously shuffling about and doing stretch exercises; he wondered if a fitness video might be a wise career move. More seriously, Yates discussed the new acceptance of hip hop at Glastonbury in the wake of Jay-Z's much-publicised appearance there in 2008, at which Dizzee reminded him that he played there first, in 2007, although he did also tell viewers that Jay-Z remained one of his idols. Finally, wondered the presenters, what would he be doing next, following such an incredibly successful year? How would he top it? One thing was for sure – a sabbatical was out of the question. "I'll never stop making music," he said.

He was similarly unlikely now to stop being a daily fixture in our lives. That summer, he was interviewed at length – these things being relative – by the *News Of The World*. There he spoke about his evolution from mentally scarred adolescent whose childhood was "so bleak he could have ended up seeing a psychiatrist" to permanently grinning mainstay of the UK hit parade. It was one of the longest, strangest pop trips of recent times. Nobody could have predicted that the Boy In Da Corner would become, within a few short years, the nation's favourite Bonkers pop star. As for what would come next, that was anyone's guess.

"I get bored really quickly. Life's a blur, because the next thought can't come quickly enough, my mind is always bubbling, bubbling, bubbling," he told the *News Of The World*. If the future seemed uncertain – a return to harsh grime, an even deeper dive into mainstream pop waters? – his present was anything but tense. "I'm dedicating my life to improving the mood," he said. "I'm bringing up the general happiness of the country. Lovely jubbly."